Old
Jews
Telling
Jokes

Old Jews Telling Jokes

5,000 Years of Funny Bits and Not–So–Kosher Laughs

SAM HOFFMAN with ERIC SPIEGELMAN

VILLARD   NEW YORK

Contents

A Note of Introduction

Old Jews Telling Jokes.

It's a simple concept, one of those ideas where the name tells you everything you need to know. Like "peanut butter" or "Dungeons & Dragons." Or "autoerotic asphyxiation."

Old Jews Telling Jokes. No-brainer, right? Let's face it—jokes are funny. Jews are funny. Old Jews—funnier still.

But, like every success story, it was an uphill climb.

Eric Spiegelman and his business partner, Tim Williams, were starting an Internet content company and they asked me if I had any ideas for a site. I said yes. I have a great one. How about a site for social networking where you could reconnect with all the people that you had spent the last twenty years trying to avoid?

They said it would never catch on.

So I pitched them my second idea. Porn. As in: pornography. We could just use the Internet to distribute naked videos of all sorts of people having sex with each other in novel and interesting ways.

They told me to stop being ridiculous.

Why would anyone want to watch porn at home when you could go to a dirty, crappy theater in a horrible part of town and watch it with a bunch of unwashed strangers?

I said fine. You guys want to be like that? Here's an idea for you. Why don't we just go videotape my dad and his friends telling the same old jokes they've been telling for forty years?

And *Old Jews Telling Jokes* was born.

All kidding aside, *Old Jews Telling Jokes* did begin in an abandoned storefront in my hometown of Highland Park, New Jersey, with a group of twenty of my father's friends and relatives. He cast people who he thought could "tell a good story," and indeed that's what it's all about. We lit the set carefully and shot against a plain white background, to indicate that these were more than jokes; they were portraits. We also decided that no joke teller could be younger than sixty years old. We wanted a lifetime of experience to infuse these jokes.

Old jokes, fairly or not, tend to be stigmatized. I think this has something to do with the way we naturally respond to humor. Things are much funnier when they surprise us; therefore the first time we hear a particular joke is probably the best time we will ever hear it. To some immeasurable extent, it lessens in value with each hearing.

Despite this, jokes, because of their ability to entertain, tend to last longer than other forms of oral communication. They get passed around and around, sometimes for decades. The jokes themselves become time capsules, revealing the fears and anxieties and celebrating the joys of all aspects of life, including its end.

Needless to say, our site became a hit. It only took me three or four days to explain to the older joke tellers that "going viral" was a good thing. As of this writing the jokes have been seen six million times. We have shot rounds of jokes in New York City and in Los Angeles, and we have plans to shoot soon in Florida and London. The beauty of shooting in Los Angeles was that Eric, a native of that city, tasked his father with putting together the cast of old Jews. I found great satisfaction in the symmetry of our two fathers, on opposite coasts, pooling friends to come preserve and celebrate these stories and jokes with us.

This book endeavors to take the process a step further. We have categorized the jokes into chapters, roughly tracing the trajectory of the Jewish experience in America. Make no mistake: We do not attempt scholarly analysis—we'll gladly leave that work in the competent hands of academics. Rather our goal is a portrait, both in photos and jokes, of an evolving culture.

Old
Jews
Telling
Jokes

1

The Jewish Mother

What? All of the Sudden You Don't Like My Brisket?

She was so deeply embedded in my consciousness that for the first year of school I seem to have believed that each of my teachers was my mother in disguise. As soon as the last bell had sounded, I would rush off for home, wondering as I ran if I could possibly make it to our apartment before she had succeeded in transforming herself. Invariably she was already in the kitchen by the time I arrived, and setting out my milk and cookies. Instead of causing me to give up my delusions, however, the feat merely intensified my respect for her powers.

So starts *Portnoy's Complaint*, Philip Roth's definitive kvetch novel of the American Jewish Mother. What's interesting to me is that Roth's portrait doesn't start with any of the petty stereotypical claims—overprotective, anxious, neurotic. Instead Portnoy's mother is defined by her power.

Coincidentally, when I posted my own mother's joke to our website, it was accompanied by the following description: "Diane Hoffman is my mom. She can do pretty much anything and, at any given time, is doing everything." The phrasing may be less sublime, but the sentiment is related. If we, and by "we" I mean the Jewish boys, have an issue with our mothers, the issue is with their abundance of gifts, talents, and abilities, or at least with our perception of these things.

But why are these Jewish mothers so exaggerated? Are there steroids in the flanken? What has created this über-race of shape-shifting moms?

Some scholars suggest that it is intrinsically tied to the Jewish suburban flight during the middle of the last century. For generations the mother had occupied the central role in the Jewish family. In the shtetl, they ran the household, which could include domesticated animals and small farming, while the fathers often spent copious time studying Torah. Suddenly these ferociously intelligent, energetic women were stuck in a house in the middle of nowhere with little or nothing to do. By the 1950s, many could even afford a little help around the house with the laundry and the dusting.

So what's a ravenously curious, intellectually gifted, ambitious woman to do? Many joined associations and community groups such as Hadassah and synagogue sisterhoods. Many ran parent-teacher organizations and started book clubs and charity organizations. And starting in the 1960s, many started to enter the labor market. But before having a job became a generally accepted option, many turned their laserlike focus to their children. This had a mixed effect, which we could address further if we had a chapter on psychoanalysis, but unfortunately the publishers didn't find our collection of 378 Freudian knock-knock jokes to be worth printing.

One might ask—why start the book with a chapter on Jewish mothers?

The answer is simple. That's where it all starts.

A Freudian Knock-Knock Joke

"Knock knock."

"Who's there?"

"Oedipus."

"Oedipus who?"

"Oedipus shmedipus, as long as he loves his mother."

DENNIS SPIEGELMAN

Dennis Spiegelman is Eric's dad. He moved to Los Angeles in 1963, married a shiksa (Eric's word choice), and had two children. He deals in antique and collectible objects.

My Son, the President

It's the year 2016, and a Jew has been elected president. He calls his mother and says, "Ma, I'm the president of the United States! Are you coming to the inauguration?"

She says, "Eh, well, I've got nothing to wear."

He says, "Ma, I'm gonna be the president. I can get you a dressmaker."

She says, "Eh, well, I only eat kosher."

"Ma, I'm gonna be president! I can get you a kosher meal."

She says, "Eh, well, how am I gonna get there?"

"Ma, I can get you Air Force One. Come to the inaugural."

She ends up at the inaugural and they're on the reviewing stand. On the left side of her are all of the Supreme Court justices; on the right side is the president's cabinet.

She nudges the guy to her right and says, "You see that guy with his hand up? His brother's a doctor!"

SYLVIE DRAKE

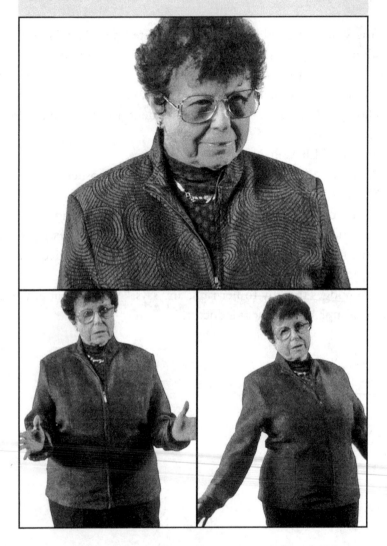

Sylvie Drake has led a fascinating life, which began in Alexandria, Egypt, in 1930. After she immigrated to the United States in 1949, she spent three years acting and directing with the Pasadena Playhouse.

Rottweiler

What is the difference between a Jewish mother and a Rottweiler?
Eventually, a Rottweiler will let go.

A Bonus Joke from Sylvie Drake

Staring at the Sea

These four women are sitting on a bench in Santa Monica.

It's a gray day. They're staring out at the gray sea, under a cloudy sky, looking miserable. They're not talking.

All of a sudden, one of them breaks the silence and says, "Oy."

Two seconds later, the one next to her says, "Oy, vey."

A few seconds later, the one next to her says, "Oy vey iz mir."

The fourth one turns toward the others and says, "Excuse me, I thought we had agreed that we weren't going to talk about the children!"

MIKE LEIDERMAN

Mike Leiderman has spent more than thirty years as a Chicago TV sportscaster, producer, writer, and host. He was so excited to be a part of *Old Jews Telling Jokes* that he flew himself from Chicago to Los Angeles to tell his jokes.

Meeting Mom

This guy tells his mother that he's finally going to get married. His mother is thrilled!

She says, "Am I gonna meet her?"

He says, "Well, Ma, I'd like to play a little game with you. You have such a good sense of what's going on. I'd like to bring in three women and have you guess which one's gonna be my wife."

His mother agrees.

The next day, he brings in three beautiful ladies and he sits down on the couch next to his mom. His mom talks to them for two minutes and says, "The redhead in the middle."

He says, "Ma, that's amazing! How'd you do that so quickly?"

She says, "'Cause I don't like her."

HAROLD ZAPOLSKY

Harold (Harry) Zapolsky spent most of his career as a professor of physics at Rutgers University, where he served two terms as department chair and is now professor emeritus. He also served in Washington, D.C., for several years as program director for theoretical physics at the National Science Foundation.

Bubele

A lady is taking her young son to his first day in school. She's walking him to school and she starts giving him a little lecture.

She says, "Now, bubele, this is a marvelous thing for you, bubele. Bubele, you're never gonna forget it. Just remember, bubele, to behave in school. Remember, bubele, anytime you want to speak, you raise your hand."

They get to the school and she says, "Bubele, have a good day. I'll be waiting for you when you get out of school."

Four hours later, she's standing there, and the little kid runs down the steps. She runs toward him and says, "Bubele, bubele, it's been such an exciting day. Tell me, bubele, what did you learn today?"

He says, "I learned my name was Irving."

Steven M. Brown, M.D.

Mothers and Sons

Three older Jewish women, sitting on a bench in Miami.

First one boasts, "I have such a wonnerful son. You know what he did for mine seventy-fifth birthday? Chartered an airplane. Got all my friends from Great Neck, flew them down here for a party at the Fontainebleau Hotel . . . in the grand ballroom! They made a chopped liver look like a svan! You could die from it! Seven-piece orchestra, we partied till two in the morning. Vhat a nize boy."

Second lady says, "Well, you have a nize son, but let me tell you about my boy. Took me around the vorld onna cruise . . . Princess Line, two whole veeks . . . Ve played shuffleboard on the deck . . . We sat at the captain's table. Parties every night. Such a great kid."

Third lady: "Vell, you have a nize boy and you have a nize boy, but let me tell you about my zon Marvin. He lives in New York City. He zees a psee-kye-a-trist [psychiatrist] tree times a veek . . . two hun'red dollars an hour . . . and all he talks about is me!!"

Sheldon Kimmelman

Hanukkah Guilt

A Jewish mother gives her son two ties on the first night of Hanukkah. The following morning, when he comes down for breakfast, he is wearing one of them.

The mom says, "What's the matter—you didn't like the other one?"

Dr. Josh Backon

Native American Wife

A guy from an Orthodox family goes out and marries a Native American girl and brings the bride home to his mother.

The bride says, "My name is Honakanaloni but you can call me Falling Water."

The mother says, "My name is Sadie Bernstein and you can call me SITTING SHIVA."

2

Who Are the Jews?

The Chosen

ANY ATTEMPT TO DESCRIBE THE JEWS BEGINS AND ENDS WITH one phrase: the Chosen.

When a Jewish boy is eight days old, his parents volunteer him for ritual surgery—some describe it as barbaric—to remove the foreskin from his penis. Later in life, if he has the good fortune to encounter a penis in its foreskin-bedecked natural state, he might turn to his parents and ask, "Why? Why does Patrick's penis have a nifty turtleneck, while mine is naked and shorn like a baby mouse?"

"Because, son, you are Chosen. Circumcision is a sign of the covenant between God and the Jewish people."

"What's a covenant?"

"A covenant is sort of a contract. A deal. Between the Jews and God."

"A deal?"

"Yes. God has chosen the Jews. In return, we get circumcised."

"I don't understand."

"Well the Jews are very lucky because there is only one god, and that god has chosen the Jews as his very favorite people. You know how you pledge allegiance to the flag in class?"

"Yes."

"Well, circumcision is sort of a pledge of allegiance to God."

"Why doesn't Patrick have to pledge allegiance to God with his penis?"

"Because Patrick is Catholic. God didn't choose them."

"Then why does he get Christmas?"

You could call the whole "Chosen" thing a mixed blessing for the Jews. For one thing, it's really kept our numbers down. Jews don't go out, door to door, like Mormons, trying to sign up more Jews. Why? It wouldn't be much of a "Chosen" club if anybody could just join. Becoming a Jew is a pain in the ass. If you don't have the required matrilineal proof of membership, you have to pass all sorts of tests and learn to read backwards. But elitism requires a small footprint.

A few generations after Abraham smashed his idols and got the Jews started, his descendants followed Joseph down into Egypt and pretty soon afterward were enslaved. (This is all covered in Genesis and Exodus, which are two parts of the Old Testament, which you can find in most motel rooms, if you want to check my facts.) They were enslaved because the Egyptians didn't trust them and thought they might join up with an enemy if Egypt were to be attacked. Why didn't the Egyptians trust them? Because they were different. They worshipped one god instead of the sun and those funny-looking cats, and they probably went around telling everyone they were Chosen.

This is the beginning of a multimillennial pattern for the Jews. They ride into town. It turns out that they are handy at doing things that the local people aren't so good at: accounting, kosher butchering, comedy. They become a useful part of the community. Then they tell the locals that they are "Chosen." This, to the locals, sounds a lot like "you idiots are specifically not Chosen." The locals get mad and kick their collective Jewish tucheses.

Now let's be fair. The Jews have been persecuted throughout the ages for a variety of sad and terrible reasons that have nothing to do with being "Chosen." But, as a result of this persecution, the Jews have adopted the tenacious pugnacity of the perpetual underdog. It's no surprise that David, slayer of the giant Goliath, is the second greatest of all Jewish mythic heroes (after Sammy Davis, Jr.).

The stories in this section illuminate this quintessential conflict at the center of the Jewish persona: the persecuted elitist, the foreskin-free pugilist, the Chosen Underdog.

RICHARD Z. CHESNOFF

Richard Z. Chesnoff was born in Brooklyn to a big-band musician father and a singer mom. Since then, in forty years of global news work, he has covered many of the major stories and personalities of our times. He has written for *Newsweek, U.S. News & World Report,* and the Huffington Post, and as an op-ed columnist for the New York *Daily News.*

A Meeting with the Pope

In the Vatican in the sixteenth century, one of the cardinals has borrowed an enormous amount of money from the Jewish banker. And he can't pay it back. So he goes to the pope and he says, "I think, Holy Father, we should get rid of all the Jews."

The pope says, "I can't throw all the Jews out. I just can't do that."

"Well," he says, "why don't you find an excuse. You challenge the rabbi to a duel over who has the truer faith."

The pope agrees, so the cardinals go to the community and talk to them. The Jews don't like the idea but they can't say no.

But one of the Jews says, "You know, our rabbi is very learned, his Hebrew is excellent, but his Italian is limited and his Latin is nonexistent. And with all due respect to the pope, I can't believe that his Hebrew is so good that he would be able to debate."

So the cardinal says, "You know what? Instead of having a debate vocally, they can debate with symbols, with signs."

So they agree. The day comes and the cardinals are assembled. The pope comes in, sits on his throne. The rabbi comes in wearing a long black robe. He sits down below. They nod to each other.

And then the pope begins. He holds up three fingers. The rabbi looks at him for a second and holds up one finger. The pope swings his finger in a circle over his head. The rabbi looks at him and points down to the ground. The pope pulls out a glass of sacramental wine and a holy wafer and holds them up. The rabbi looks at him a moment, sticks his hand in his pocket, and pulls out an apple and holds it up.

The pope slaps his hands together and says, "That's it. These Jews are too smart for me. They don't have to leave; they can stay."

The Jews exit, very happy, and the cardinals run around the pope and say, "What happened?"

"Well, I held up the sign of the Trinity—the Father, the Son, and the Holy Ghost—and the rabbi held up a sign that there's only one God. I spun my finger to say God is everywhere and he pointed down to indicate God is right here.

"I held up the sacrament, the wine, and the wafer, to show that in our faith you can, through confession and communion, relieve yourself of all sins. And he held up an apple, which indicates that you can't get rid of original sin. It's always there.

"They're just too smart."

Back in the synagogue, the Jews are dancing and celebrating and they go to the rabbi and say, "What happened?"

The rabbi says, "Can you imagine the chutzpah? This guy holds up three fingers to say, 'You've got three days to leave,' and so I give him the finger. He spins his finger over his head to say, 'You're going to leave not only from Rome but from all of Italy,' so I point down to say we're staying right here.

"And then for some reason he takes out his lunch, so I take out mine."

David Benkin

Lottery Ticket

An old Jew was sitting in shul one Shabbos.

He was praying: "Dear God, let me win the lottery just once. It would make me so very happy."

The next week he was back again: "Dear God, I'm the guy who last Shabbos asked you to let me win the lottery. I have kept all your commandments and performed all the required mitzvahs. Just this once I would like to win the lottery. Please."

He was back again the following week: "God, I have to confess, I'm getting a little annoyed. Here I am, a pious and prayerful Jew who goes to shul regularly and does everything he is supposed to do. Why won't you grant me this one favor and allow me to win the lottery."

Just then there was a clap of thunder, the roof of the shul rolled back, a bright light descended on the old fellow, and a deep voice boomed out: "Abram, Abram, meet me halfway: *Buy a ticket!*"

LOU CHARLOFF

Lou Charloff was born in Romania and moved to New York (specifically, the Bronx) when he was two years old. He speaks five languages and served as an interpreter for the military government of occupied Germany after World War II. Four years ago he decided to try his hand at stand-up comedy in Los Angeles, making him, simultaneously, one of the oldest and one of the newest comics in the business.

Herschel the Magnificent Jew

A long time ago, I was in basic training in the army. I had the day off, and I went into Kansas City. I saw a sign, and the sign said, "Tonight, 8 P.M. at the Parkway Theatre, come see Herschel the Magnificent Jew."

So, of course, I was curious. I went, and there was a good-sized crowd in the theater. At eight o'clock, they introduced him: "Ladies and gentlemen, Mr. Herschel."

He came out wearing a bathrobe. He removed his bathrobe, and he was perfectly naked. Completely naked.

Now, imagine, if you will, the largest, most masculine equipment you can think of. Herschel was four times bigger. He had a bench in front of him, and he put three walnuts on the bench. He took his masculinity in his hand, and he went whap, whap, whap! And he smashed them to smithereens. The audience applauded. When they were leaving the theater, they were still applauding.

Twenty years later—twenty years later!—I was again in Kansas City and I saw the same sign: "Tonight, 8 P.M. at the Parkway Theatre, come see Herschel the Magnificent Jew."

Well, of course I went, and it was the same thing: They introduced him, he came out, he took off his bathrobe. He looked exactly the same; hadn't changed one iota!

He put on the bench three coconuts. One, two, three. He took his masculinity in his hands and went whap, whap, whap! Smashed them to smithereens!

Well, naturally, I went backstage—I was curious. I said, "Mr. Herschel, why did you switch from walnuts to coconuts?"

He said, "Well . . . my eyesight ain't what it used to be."

MICHAEL P. KING

Michael King grew up in Las Vegas, the son of a violinist. He moved to Los Angeles to study at UCLA and attended law school at Loyola University. He has been selected as a Southern California "Super Lawyer" by *Los Angeles* magazine for each of the past three years. He has four children and six grandchildren.

Moishe Gets Knighted

Moishe, the tailor, is in London. He's been in London his whole life, and he has made all of the clothes for all of the royalty for all of England.

One day he comes home and tells his children, "You're not going to believe this, but our queen is going to make me a knight."

"Oh, Papa, that's wonderful! Our queen is going to make you a— but wait, Papa, the queen can't make you a knight."

Moishe says, "Why is that?"

"Because you have to speak Latin to the queen, and you don't know any Latin!"

"Oh, my children," he says. "We'll figure it out."

So he goes to the church, takes out a book, and reads and memorizes the Latin in the book.

The night comes when all of the knights-to-be will be made knights by the queen. Moishe goes to Prince Albert Hall and the queen is sitting on her throne at the end of a long red-carpeted aisle.

Each knight puts one knee down, and then the other knee. The queen takes the sword and puts it on one shoulder, and then the other shoulder.

"Arise, Sir John! Arise, Sir Charles!" The knights look at the queen and say this beautiful phrase in Latin.

Now it's Moishe's turn. He's walking down the aisle—all the way down the red carpet—and he puts one knee down, and the sword goes on his shoulder. He puts the other knee down, and the sword goes on his other shoulder. He stands up, and he completely forgets what he's supposed to say. The only thing he can think of—in the only foreign language he knows—is "Mah nishtana ha'leilah hazeh, mikol ha'leilot."

The queen looks at him, looks around, then says, "Why is this knight different from all the other knights?"

FRED RUBIN

Fred Rubin was born and raised in Chicago. For twenty-three years he wrote and produced network television sitcoms, working on such classics as *Diff'rent Strokes, Night Court,* and *Archie Bunker's Place.* He is currently an assistant professor at UCLA in the department of theater, film, and television.

New York Athletic Club

Bernie, an old Jew who has spent many years in the clothing business, is retiring. His friends ask him, "What're you gonna do after you retire?"

He says, "I think I'll go down and join the New York Athletic Club."

They say, "Bernie, what are you, crazy? They'll never let a Jew in there!"

And he says, "Well, I have my ways. I think I can get in."

Sure enough, after Bernie retires, he puts on a blue blazer with gold buttons, a pin-striped shirt, red silk tie, khaki Dockers, and boat shoes, and goes down to the New York Athletic Club to interview. He gets taken into a sumptuous room and a well-dressed elegant man comes out to interview him. The man sits down opposite Bernie and says, "Your name, sir?"

He says, "Ah, yes. It's Bernard Throckmorten, the Third."

The interviewer writes it down. "And what line of work are you in, sir?"

Bernie says, "Well, yes, I'm retired now, but for many years I had a small boutique advertising agency on Park Avenue."

The interviewer writes that down. "Are you married, sir? Do you have children?"

"Yes, my wife Mary does quite a bit of work for the Junior League. I have two children: Buffy and Chip. They will be matriculating this year at Harvard and Yale, respectively."

He says, "I see, sir. And your religion?"

"Ah, yes, we're goyim."

LARRY GREENFIELD

Larry Greenfield is a native of Trenton and a graduate of Princeton University. He has three children and one grandchild. He lives in New York, with the love of his life, Robin, and manages computer systems for the Metropolitan Transportation Authority. Greenfield was once a civil engineer, and he holds two patents, one of which is on a wheel. (And they said it couldn't be reinvented!)

Sidney the Lumberjack

Sidney, who's almost ninety years old, weighs maybe a hundred pounds soaking wet, walks up behind the head lumberjack, taps him on the shoulder, and says, "Excuse me, I'd like a job chopping down trees."

The lumberjack, six foot four, 275 pounds of muscle, turns around and looks at skinny, little old Sidney, and says, "You've got to be kidding. This is a tough job. Not for little old men like you. Besides, where did you ever work before chopping down trees?"

"Well, I'll have you know," says Sidney, "I used to work at the Sahara Forest."

The lumberjack looks at him and says, "You mean the Sahara Desert?"

"Oh, well, *now!*"

ALAN KESSLER

Alan Kessler, born in Brooklyn, is the CEO of an international Japanese construction and real estate company. He also paints and practices photography.

A Trip to Miami

So Irving is sitting at home reading the *Forvitz* and he sees a little ad that says "Round-trip cruise to Miami, $35."

And he sees a phone number there, so he picks up the phone and he calls the number and the guy answers and he says, "Is this for real?"

"Yes, this is for real."

"Well, what do I do?"

"When do you want to go?"

"I'll go tomorrow."

"Well, you just pack a little bag, you stand in front of your building, and we'll pick you up and take you to the boat."

So Irving packs a little bag, and the next morning he stands in front of his building. Up pulls a van. Two big guys get out, they grab Irving, they throw him in the van. They take his little bag, they throw it in the van, they drive to the Hudson River, pier 36. They take Irving out, they schlep him out onto the pier, they put him into a galley ship and tie him to an oar.

Suddenly, this big guy comes out with a whip and he starts whipping everybody and they start to row. He's yelling, "Row!" and he's whipping them.

This goes on for three days, the rowing and the whipping, and finally they're pulling into the port of Miami.

Irving turns to the guy next to him and says, "You ever do this before?"

"I do it every year."

"Well, maybe you can tell me something."

"What's that?"

"How much do you tip the whipper?"

MICHAEL MILLER

Michael Miller is a television and documentary writer/producer and practical joker. He's been an Angeleno, a New Yorker, and a Buffalonian. A lifetime appreciator of Jewish humor, since long before his bar mitzvah, he learned about sex from Belle Barth and life from Lenny Bruce. Or maybe it was vice versa.

Desert Island

This man has been stranded on a desert island for many, many years. Every day he goes out to the beach and looks out on the horizon, looking for some action.

One day he sees a steamer in the distance. He's so excited! It's the first sign of life he's seen in years. He builds a little fire by the shore and throws some leaves on it, so there'll be smoke rising. He starts jumping around, waving his hands.

Sure enough, the steamer stops, turns, and starts heading toward him. He's so thrilled! He sees the small lifeboat come off, six guys jump in it, and they're paddling to him.

He runs out to meet them. "I'm so happy you came here."

They say, "Sir, we'll take you wherever you want to go. We're here to save you."

He says, "That's great, but first I want to show you my island. I've lived here many years, so I've done a few things to it." He shows them the grove of fruit trees that he's planted from the seeds of fruits that have washed ashore. He shows them his house, a little shack, which he's built and lived in. He takes them to another shed and says, "This is my synagogue. This is where I pray."

One of the guys looks around and sees that there's another shed in the distance. He says, "What's that over there?"

He says, "That's the other synagogue. I don't go there."

RICHARD LEVINE

Richard Levine was born in Brooklyn (a hotbed of talent for joke tellers of this generation). He is semiretired from his business of printing forms and labels for clinical drug studies for the pharmaceutical industry. He has permanently relocated from New Jersey to West Palm Beach, Florida.

Directions

A woman calls up her friend. She says, "Becky, I understand you got a new apartment."

Becky says, "I do. I got a pretty apartment. Why don't you come visit?"

"I'd love to visit, but I don't know where you live. You gotta give me directions."

"I live on 1486 Eighty-sixth Street. You'll take the train, get off at Eighty-sixth Street. You'll see a big apartment complex, 1486. Outside, you'll see a double door. With your right elbow, press down the handle from the door, push open the door, and you'll be in what we call a vestibule.

"In the vestibule's a list of bells. I'm apartment 4B. With the left elbow, press 4B; it'll ring upstairs. As soon as I hear the ring, I'll buzz you.

"When you hear the buzz, with your right elbow press on the inside of the door, push open the door, go straight ahead to the elevator, and with the left elbow press UP.

"You'll get in the elevator; with the right elbow press 4 for the fourth floor. The door will open up; you'll go straight into my apartment, 4B.

"You'll ring the doorbell with the right elbow. Give it a couple of knocks with the left elbow; I'll answer the door. You'll come in; we'll have coffee."

Her friend interrupts, fed up. "What kind of directions are these, with the elbow? The left elbow, the right elbow. What's with the elbow?"

Becky says, "What? You're coming empty-handed?"

LAWRENCE GOLDBERG

Lawrence Goldberg was born in Detroit and learned most of his favorite jokes from his aunt, who frequently visited his family's apartment with new material.

Two Beggars in Rome

Two beggars were sitting outside the Tivoli fountain in Rome. One beggar had his hat in front of him, decorated with a crucifix. The other had his hat in front of him, his with a Star of David.

People are walking by, and they're all putting their donations into the hat with the crucifix.

A priest walks by, and he sees the two of them sitting there, and he says, "My good man, this is a Catholic city. No one's going to put money in a hat with a Star of David! As a matter of fact, most Catholics and Christians in this city will probably donate extra to the hat with the crucifix."

The beggar with the Star of David turns to the other and says, "Moshe, look who's trying to tell the Cohen brothers about marketing!"

DENNIS SPIEGELMAN

Dennis Spiegelman grew up in Buffalo, New York, and has fond memories of spending summers at Crystal Beach on Lake Erie. Whenever he goes back to visit, he picks up dozens of bottles of loganberry juice, which was invented at the Crystal Beach Amusement Park in the late nineteenth century and is mostly unavailable outside the area.

Bra Shopping

Sam goes into Macy's, to the lingerie department, and he says to the salesgirl, "My wife has sent me in for a Jewish bra, size 34B, and she said that you'd know what I meant."

The saleslady says, "Boy, it's been a long time since anybody's asked me for a Jewish bra. They usually ask me for a Catholic bra or a Salvation Army bra or a Presbyterian bra."

He says, "Well, what's the difference?"

She says, "The Catholic bra supports the masses, the Salvation Army bra uplifts the downfallen, and the Presbyterian bra keeps them staunch and upright."

He goes, "Well, then what's a Jewish bra?"

"Oh, a Jewish bra makes mountains out of molehills."

FRED RUBIN

Fred Rubin's career accomplishments include a stint as a rock-and-roll columnist, time spent as a social worker, and a job as a singing waiter.

Air-Conditioning

Around the 1920s, three Jewish brothers invent this miraculous machine that can instantly cool a room. It's not like a fan, which blows hot air around. It literally sucks in hot air and blows out cold air. They want to market it; they want to do something with it, but they don't know what to do. They decide to take it to Henry Ford, the great industrialist, never knowing that he's a radical anti-Semite.

They take the machine to Ford. He says, "Well, plug it in. Let's see it work." They plug it in and instantly the room gets cool. Henry Ford's eyes light up, and he says, "I want this. I want this machine. I'll give you a million dollars for it right now!"

The Schwartzman brothers say, "All right! We're happy with that, but we want the name Schwartzman on it, in big letters!"

Henry Ford goes, "Oh no, that's impossible. I can't do that, but I'll make you a deal: I'll give you two million dollars, but no way's 'Schwartzman' on the machine, no way."

They go, "No, you know, we're proud. Proud of the work we did. Proud of our heritage. We're proud of our name. It's got to have our name on it."

Henry Ford says, "No, no, I can't. Tell you what: I'll give you three million dollars, but no name on it."

Well, this kind of intrigues them. It's a lot of money. They talk it over, and they propose a compromise to Henry Ford, and he agrees.

That is why, to this day, on every air conditioner it says, "Norm Hi Max."

Dr. Josh Backon

Christmas

It's a second-grade class in an American public school. The teacher asks each child to tell the others how he will celebrate Christmas.

Johnnie says, "I help my daddy cut down a tree."

Susie says, "I help decorate the tree."

Christopher says, "I like to open the presents."

Then it's Moishe's turn.

He says, "We all climb into my father's Rolls-Royce. We drive over to his toy factory. My father looks at the empty shelves and says, 'Thank you, Jesus!' and then we all fly to the Bahamas for a week's vacation!"

3

Coming to America

Fighting for Elbow Room on the Lower East Side

THE JEWS ARRIVED IN AMERICA ESSENTIALLY IN THREE BATCHES. The first batch were the Sephardim. The second batch, also known as the fancy-shmancy, German Jewish batch, came to New York during the 1840s and '50s. The third batch, the shtetl (village) Jews of Russia, Poland, and other parts of Eastern Europe, emigrated in large numbers between 1880 and 1920.

The Sephardim were Jews of Iberian descent who arrived in New Amsterdam in the middle of the seventeenth century. They founded the first American synagogue, the Touro, in Newport, Rhode Island. It was completed in 1763. The Sephardim will not be mentioned again in this book because they are not funny.

The German Jews were already urbanized, educated, enlightened, and sophisticated before they came to the United States. In New York, they moved quickly uptown and founded grand palaces of worship such as Temple Emanu-el and Central Synagogue. They did business and assimilated into American society. They founded "Reform Judaism" and intellectual institutions such as the Society for Ethical Culture as a way of distancing themselves from some of the more annoying elements of Judaism, such as keeping kosher, keeping the Sabbath, and believing in God.

Of course, the German Jews were appalled when the shtetl Jews fled the Russian pogroms and started showing up on Orchard Street. Not only were they Russian or (even worse) Polish, they were dirty and poor. They wore big bushy beards and peasant costumes and they reminded other Americans about the nasty historical stereotype of the Jew—one that the German Jews had been diligently working for decades to eradicate. The uptown Jews called these more recent arrivals "greenhorns." The new arrivals called the uptown Jews "goyim."

The wave of emigration from Eastern Europe brought Jews to many American cities, including Philadelphia, Newark, Baltimore, Boston, and Chicago. But many more came to New York. There many of the greenhorns were clustered in the Lower East Side, shoulder to shoulder with (gasp) gentiles—recent arrivals from Ireland, Italy, Poland, Ukraine, and Germany, as well as Chinese. The Lower East Side epitomized the "melting pot" of pre–World War I America. Where else in the world could you get the three P's—pickles, pierogi, and prosciutto—in a three-block radius?

For the recent arrivals this was a time both of great anxiety and awe-inspiring opportunity. America, unlike Europe, placed no constraints upon the Jews' entrepreneurial spirit and many started professional, manufacturing, and retailing businesses that became stalwarts of the American economy. But new, terrifying experiences lurked around every American corner. Many of these folks had never seen anything but their village, a train, a boat, and Ellis Island. Who were these Italians on Mulberry Street with their giant cured hams? Who were these Chinese on Grand Street with their ducks hanging in the window? Who were these Protestants uptown and why did they buy retail?

From the time of their arrival and through the Great Depression and the World War II years, the American Jewish experience was urban. The city cradled and suckled the first generations of American-born Jews and transitioned the culture from greenhorn to apple-pie-noshing American. The jokes that follow capture the excitement and fear of that experience.

ARCHIE BARKAN

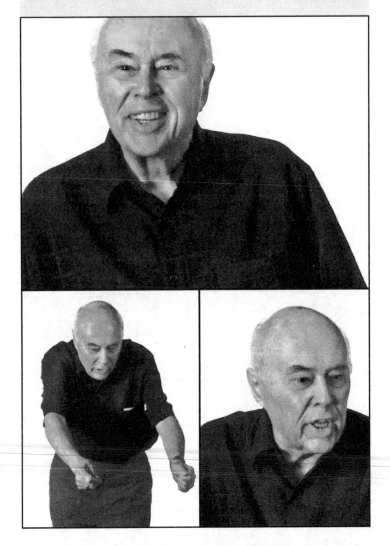

Archie Barkan is a professor of Yiddish at Emeritus College in Santa Monica, California, and was once a tummler at the Stevensville Hotel in the Catskills and at Tamiment in the Poconos.

Mrs. Nafkawitz

So, at the shtetl in the old country, the Jews lived with a certain kind of decorum, and they wouldn't go, for instance, to a saloon to drink, but it didn't mean they didn't have a few drinks at home.

The shtetl had a "lady of the evening"—the Yiddish word is *nafka*—and she walked the streets with her nice purse. She had this nice, light dress on.

And everybody, in Yiddish, they say, "Macht zikh nit visndik"—they pay her no mind. She did her thing, and they didn't call her nafka, but they called her "Mrs. Nafkawitz," with that kind of decorum they had.

Nineteen twenty came, and everybody moved out of the city. They migrated to New York, and everything was wonderful.

Ten years later, one guy made a fortune. He's got a good heart, he wants to share his good fortunes with somebody from the shtetl, and . . . they've all disappeared! He can't find anybody.

Suddenly, one day, he's walking on Forty-second Street—big, wide street that it is—and he sees her on the other side of the street. Even her, he's so happy to see somebody from the shtetl! He yells out, "Mrs. Nafkawitz!"

She says, "Shh! Here in America, they call me 'Horowitz'!"

JERRY FISHER

Rabbi Jerry Fisher was born in Chicago and came to Los Angeles as a teenager. He graduated from Hamilton High School, and UCLA with a degree in psychology. While completing his bachelor of Hebrew letters degree at the Los Angeles School of the Hebrew Union College, he served as student-rabbi of Temple Solael in Canoga Park.

Chaim Ginsburg Chinese Laundry

A guy's walking around New York's Lower East Side and he passes by a Chinese laundry. It says CHAIM GINSBURG CHINESE LAUNDRY and he looks inside and sees this Chinese guy.

He says, "I don't understand. Who's Chaim Ginsburg?"

The guy says, "I'm Chaim Ginsburg."

He says, "Well, where did you get a name like Chaim Ginsburg?"

The guy says, "I was standing in line at Ellis Island, and there was a Jewish guy in front of me.

"The Jewish guy was asked, 'What's your name?' and he says, 'My name is Chaim Ginsburg,' and they wrote it down.

"Then they asked me, 'Next in line, okay, what's your name?'

"I said, 'Sam Ting.' "

EILEEN LOTTMAN

Eileen Lottman spent her adolescence in Sioux City, Iowa, during World War II, cheering up Army Air Forces personnel who were stationed at a base in town.

Insufficient Passage

Abie and Becky had been married for several years, and there was no sign of a baby. So they were very upset, and Abie told Becky to go to the doctor and ask him what's the matter.

So she went to the doctor, and the doctor examined her. And he said, "Well, you have an insufficient passage, and if you have a baby, it'll be a miracle."

So she went home and Abie says, "Nu, nu? What did the doctor say?"

"The doctor said I got a fish in the passage and if I have a baby it'll be a mackerel."

A Note from Eileen Lottman Regarding the "Greenhorn" Joke

My mother was born in 1902 in Minneapolis, which made her a born Yankee, thanks to my grandfather's early decision to get the hell out of Lithuania. A major perk of being a Yankee was that you got to laugh at the hilarious mistakes made by the newer arrivals— greenhorns—as they poured off the boats and began trying to learn American ways and a whole new language. The humor was benign and once the greenhorns became Yankees (albeit mit a Yiddish haccent), they too began to tell "Abie and Becky stories." Now the stories have been passed down to us and our kids and their kids and the greenhorn jokes have a very special nostalgic place in Jewish American culture.

PAUL EISENMAN

Paul Eisenman was born in the Bronx but moved as a young adult to New Jersey, where he did news reporting and editing of newspapers. More than fifty years ago he established an advertising and PR agency, Eisenman-Todd, where he found an outlet for his political passions by becoming a specialist in campaigns. After the 2004 election, he cofounded Bergen Grassroots, which he currently chairs.

A Tourist in New York City

A tourist in New York City walks up to a New Yorker.

He says to the guy, "Excuse me, sir, could you direct me to the Statue of Liberty or should I just go fuck myself?"

Sharon Eisbrenner

Syphilis

There was a little old Jewish man who was having trouble with his private parts.

His wife nudged him to go to the doctor to find out what was wrong. After a lot of nudging, he finally went, and was surprised when the doctor told him he had syphilis. All the way home on the bus he kept thinking, Syphilis? What is this syphilis?

When he got home his wife said, "Nu, Hymie, what did the doctor say?"

Hymie shrugged his shoulders and said, "I don't know, he told me something, syphilis, I don't know what it is."

His wife said, "Wait—I'll look it up in the medical dictionary."

When she came back she said, "Hymie, we got nothing to worry about. It's a disease of the gentiles."

Morty Ballin

Chinese Waiter

Sam and his wife, Sadie, were visiting New York City from Cleveland.

Around lunchtime one day, they found themselves in the Garment District and went into a kosher restaurant, called Ben Siegel's.

They sat down in a booth and were approached by a Chinese waiter.

They thought this was odd, but were astonished when the waiter took their order, speaking perfect Yiddish.

During the meal, when Ben Siegel came around to their table to ask if everything was all right, Sam mentioned to him how surprised they were that the Chinese waiter spoke such good Yiddish.

"Shh," said Ben. "He thinks I'm teaching him English."

4

Moving to the Suburbs

Success!

IN THE YEARS AFTER WORLD WAR II, THE CITY BEGAN TO LOSE some of its luster. The economy was booming and the Jews had a few shekels in their pockets. Families were growing, and three or four kids, plus Grandma Sophie, was a tight squeeze in a railroad apartment. With Levittown and other suburbs beckoning only a short train ride from the city, Jews grabbed their own lot-sized parcels of American terra firma.

To have a house was to partake fully in the American dream, but it meant so much more. For one thing, suburban non-Jews could now stare at jars of gefilte fish in the local Stop & Shop and wonder, Where the hell do you catch one of those?

If the cities were a half-step from the homogeneous God-fearing life of the European shtetls, then the suburbs were another world entirely. The Jews, by choice and because of discrimination, tended to stick to proven "Jewish" suburbs, but their assimilation into American culture was deepening still. A new culture began to seep into the society: the worship of "success."

While their neighbors were keeping up with the Joneses, the Jews were defining their own rules of conspicuous consumption. Social status could be codified by any of numerous possessions: membership in synagogues and golf clubs, lavish bar mitzvahs, overachieving children, cosmetic surgery, winters in Florida, groovy 3-D prints by Agam, or even braided gold chains with really bulky chais.

Success and its trappings brought mixed feelings to the Jews. Is it kosher to miss shul on Saturday if you shoot three under par? Can you eat bacon at your beach house if the renters are just going to do it anyway? Is it okay to drive a Mercedes even though it's made by Germans? The jokes in this chapter give voice to those feelings.

MAX WEISBERG

Max Weisberg was born in Cleveland, lived in Los Angeles for forty-five years, and now resides in Scottsdale, Arizona. He once donated a collection of Jewish folklore and humor books to the library at the University of Judaism in Los Angeles.

Moving to Beverly Hills

There was this couple that was very successful. They used to be in the scrap metal business—junk business—in Boyle Heights, California. They became prosperous and moved to Beverly Hills.

One night, the husband says to the wife, "Becky, listen, how's about a bite to eat?"

She says, "Morris, please, in Boyle Heights you'd say 'How's about a bite to eat?' In Beverly Hills you'd say, 'How's about a snack?' "

"Fine. How's about a snack?" He makes her something, and they finish. "Becky, how's about we go for a walk?"

She says, "Morris, please, in Boyle Heights you'd say, 'How's about we go for a walk?' In Beverly Hills you'd say, 'How's about we go for a stroll?' "

"Fine, let's go for a stroll." So, they go for a stroll. They come back. He says, "Becky, how's about we go for a schtup?"

She says, "Morris, in Boyle Heights you'd say, 'How's about we go for a schtup?' In Beverly Hills you'd say, 'Let's go to the party.' "

He says, "Let's go to the party."

They're in bed, they're doing their thing, they're hocking away at each other. He turns to her and says, "Becky, are you coming yet?"

She says, "Morris, in Boyle Heights you'd say, 'Are you coming yet?' In Beverly Hills, you'd say, 'Are you sailing yet?' "

He says, "Becky, are you sailing yet?"

She says, "Morris, I'm not sailing yet." They go on a bit longer.

"Becky, are you sailing yet?"

"No, Morris, I'm not sailing yet."

They go some more, some more.

"Becky, are you sailing yet?"

"No, Morris, I'm not sailing yet."

"Becky! I'm sailing, I'm leaving the party, bon voyage!"

Sam Shannon

The Bar Mitzvah

Murray was planning a bar mitzvah for his son, like nothing anyone had ever seen. Invitees would be flown first-class to Africa and mounted on elephants to trudge through remote jungles to an extraordinary, beautiful savannah where the ceremony would be held.

The procession ambled through dense brush for hours until suddenly it was held up. Nobody in the back could see the problem, so they called forward, elephant to elephant, to see what the holdup was.

The answer came back, relayed rider to rider, all the way to the rear of the procession.

"We had to stop! There's another bar mitzvah up ahead."

Gershon Evan

The Son-in-Law

A young woman tells her mom that she thinks she's pregnant. Very worried, the mother goes to the drugstore and buys a pregnancy kit. The test result shows that the girl is indeed going to have a baby. Shouting and crying, the mother says, "Who did this to you? I need to know!"

The girl picks up the phone and makes a call. Half an hour later, a Ferrari stops in front of their house. A distinguished-looking man, impeccably dressed in an Armani suit, steps out of a Ferrari and enters the house.

He sits in the living room with the father, mother, and young woman and tells them, "Your daughter has informed me of the situation. I can't marry her because of my personal family situation, but I'll take responsibility. I'll cover all of her expenses and provide for your daughter for the rest of her life.

"Additionally, if a girl is born, I will bequeath her a Ferrari, a beach house, two retail stores, a town house, a beachfront villa, and two million dollars in cash.

"If a boy is born, my legacy will be a few factories and four million dollars.

"If it's twins, they will receive a factory and two million dollars each.

"However, if there is a miscarriage, what do you suggest I do?"

At this point, the father, who has remained silent, places a hand firmly on the man's shoulder and tells him, "You try again."

LARRY ZICKLIN

Larry Zicklin is a clinical professor at New York University's Stern School of Business. Before retiring, he was managing partner at Neuberger Berman.

Generosity

Max is at his golf club. He's finished playing a round, showered and shaved, and is now getting dressed. The cellphone next to him rings; it's on speaker. The voice on the other end says, "Honey, you there?"

"Yes."

"Honey, you remember that mink coat I wanted to buy, but it was a little too expensive? The furrier called today. Instead of $18,000, he's willing to give it to me for $16,500 and I bought it. I hope you don't mind."

"You loved it. I'm glad you bought it."

"Also, the Mercedes. The auto dealer called. In this economy, he wants to get rid of his inventory. Instead of $86,000, it's $78,000.

"Can you get it with all the options?"

"All the options."

"Buy it."

"And those three French dresses that I really wanted, that will last me the entire winter? Eleven thousand dollars. I hope you don't mind."

"It's okay if you want it."

"Thank you. You're so generous, dear."

Max hangs up and finishes dressing. Everyone in the locker room is amazed that he's been so generous with his wife.

As he's leaving, he turns to the locker room and says, "Anyone know who owns this cellphone?"

ED KOCH

Ed Koch was the mayor of New York City from 1977 through 1989. When I asked him if he would tell a joke for the site, he responded, "I don't tell jokes. I tell anecdotes." Always quick on my feet, I said, "You can do whatever you'd like, Mr. Mayor."

Campaign Stop

I ran for mayor in 1977, and as I ran around town talking to people to encourage them to support me, I met with a group of two hundred elderly senior citizens, Jewish, in the Bronx.

I was late. I had been in other parts of the city, and when I got to the Bronx, they were still waiting. It was ten o'clock at night.

And when I walked in, there were some who were a little upset wondering how they were gonna get home that night without being mugged.

I said to them, "I don't have to tell you what the issue in this campaign is. You know it as well as I. It's crime. Crime. And do you know that a judge that I know was mugged this week? And he called a press conference. And he said to those reporters, 'This mugging will in no way affect my decisions and judgment in matters of this nature.' "

And an elderly lady in the back of the room stood up and said, "Then mug him again."

Mitch Green

(as told to him by his grandfather Al Scaduto)

The Golden Toilet

A couple is invited to a swanky dinner party. When they arrive, they are blown away: The mansion is immaculate, the wine is free-flowing, the food is top-notch, everything is perfect.

Toward the end of the night, when everyone has consumed a fair share of wine, the husband excuses himself to go to the bathroom.

When he gets back, he tells his wife, "Sadie, I knew the people who lived here were rich, but you have no idea!"

Sadie replies, "What do you mean?"

"The bathroom, you have to see it, they have golden toilets! Literally made of gold!"

Sadie doesn't believe her husband and refuses to go to the bathroom just to look at the toilets. The night goes on and Sadie's husband keeps insisting that she go to look.

They eventually leave, without Sadie going to look, but the next morning, Sadie's husband is still going on and on about the golden toilet. Sadie finally gives in and decides they will go back to the mansion to look at the toilet. When the couple arrives at the mansion, they ring the doorbell and the butler answers.

continued

Sadie says, "I am so sorry to interrupt your day, but is the missus of the house available?"

The missus comes to the door and asks, "How can I help you?"

Sadie, extremely apologetic, starts talking. "I'm sorry to be rude, but my husband and I were here last night for the party, which was amazing! Thank you for hosting it; it was great. There is just one thing, though. My husband keeps insisting that you had a golden toilet, and I just had to see it for myself."

The missus of the house takes a long look at Sadie and her husband, turns around, and yells out, "Hey Morty, I know who shit in your tuba!"

JIM ROSENTHAL

James Rosenthal was born in Buenos Aires, Argentina. At the age of nine, Jimmy and his family set sail for the United States and settled in Brooklyn. After attending Brooklyn College, Jimmy entered the paint manufacturing business and ran a successful industrial paint company.

The Treatment

This lady is going out with her husband for a good day and he says to her, "Sadie, what's the matter? You look unhappy."

She says, "Well, I'd like to have bigger breasts and I don't know what to do; we can't afford plastic surgery."

"You want bigger breasts?" he says.

"Yes."

He says, "Well, I've got the secret. You take a roll of toilet paper and you rub it on your chest for five days."

"What's that gonna do?"

"I don't know, but it worked on your ass."

5

The Rabbi

And You Shouldn't Forget the Mohel

THE RABBI! THE RABBI! TRADITION!

Can't you just see that sweet little bearded rabbi in *Fiddler on the Roof* sagaciously intoning "May the lord bless and keep the czar . . . far away from us"? Tradition!

That's when being a rabbi was being a rabbi!

There was no Internet. There were no condo boards. There were no therapists!

You had a question? Talk to the rabbi. You had a problem with your neighbor? Talk to the rabbi. You weren't sure if the chicken was kosher? Talk to the rabbi. You were depressed?

Talk to the rabbi.

Rabbis were like super-Jews. If you think Jews can be know-it-alls, the rabbis knew more than all of them. They had the keys to the kingdom. They got to be wise, pious, and respected, but, unlike their Catholic counterparts, they didn't have to take a vow of chastity. They had it all and good lovin' too!

But what's in it for a rabbi today? Have MAO inhibitors basically undermined the need for faith-based counseling? Does the modern American Jew ever think to him or herself, Man, this is a sticky problem. I better go ask my rabbi about it.

I spoke to my cousin, Rabbi Andy Busch, about this. He's not the only rabbi I know, but he's the only rabbi whose father tells a joke in this book. He told me, as you might expect, that rabbis are still pretty busy.

While the therapists, counselors, and lawyers we see on a daily basis are all specialists, a rabbi can offer the benefit of being a generalist. The rabbi's wider perspective includes not only some training in counseling, but also larger issues of community, ethics, and Jewish tradition. He or she is not a "professional stranger" like your shrink but rather a part of your life—someone who just celebrated the birth of your child or presided over the memorial service of a relative.

Yeah, I thought to myself, but you're still a rabbi. And by that I mean, aren't you going to make me feel guilty about not coming to temple on Shemini Atzeret or Simchas Torah?

Andy said no. He doesn't do that. On purpose, at least.

But what of the mohel—the Master of the Shnip, the King of the Cut, the Prince of the Putz? Well, they never have to worry about their business.

Why?

Because they work for tips!

JOEL LEIZER

Joel Leizer runs an extremely busy dental practice and is a former president of the New Jersey Dental Association. He is an avid golfer and a proud grandfather, and his favorite time for a dental appointment is two-thirty.

Oy. I know. Sorry.

Pork

There's an old rabbi who wants to try eating pork before he dies. Being an orthodox rabbi, he can't go ahead and eat pork in his community. So he decides to travel to a restaurant about fifty miles away.

He goes into the restaurant, and on the menu is a dish called suckling pig. So he orders the suckling pig. And they bring it out on a beautiful, beautiful tray, with an apple in its mouth.

Just as he's about to take his first bite, in walks Goldberg, the president of his congregation. Goldberg says, "Rabbi! What are you doing, what are you eating?"

The rabbi says, "Goldberg, can you believe this restaurant? I order a baked apple, this is how they serve it to me."

BARNETT HOFFMAN

Barnett Hoffman, my dad, was a criminal judge in New Jersey for twenty years and would occasionally crack jokes from the bench. (Lawyers were not required to laugh but the smart ones did.) He was also the original casting director for this project.

Questions for the Rabbi

A gentile fellow who is going to marry a very ultra-Orthodox Jewish woman goes to see the ultra-Orthodox rabbi who converted him. It is the night before the wedding and the rabbi says to him, "Now, do you have any questions about tomorrow for the wedding?"

"Yes, Rabbi, as a matter of fact I do. Tomorrow night, at the wedding, can I dance with my wife?"

"Absolutely not. The men dance with the men. The women dance with the women."

"How about eating?"

"Absolutely not. You cannot eat with your wife. The men eat with the men. The women eat with the women. Do you have any other questions?"

"Well, Rabbi, while I have you here can I ask you some questions about sexual issues?"

"Sure, ask whatever you want."

"Rabbi, with regard to positions: with the man on the top, the woman on the bottom, the missionary position."

"Well, we don't call it that, but, it's okay."

"How about with the woman on top and the man on bottom?"

"It's a little different, but there's nothing wrong with that."

"How about doggy style?"

"Ooh, that's a little kinky, but there's nothing in Halacha that prevents it. Any other questions?"

"Yes, Rabbi, one last question: How about doing it standing up?"

"Absolutely not. That could lead to dancing."

MIKE LEIDERMAN

When Mike Leiderman worked for NewsCenter5 in Chicago in the 1970s, he "had a reputation for coming up with some tricky off-the-wall stories," including one about a seventy-three-year-old California Angels coach who once roomed with Babe Ruth.

Stuck on the Toilet

Abie and Becky are in bed and, of course, Abie always leaves the seat up when he goes to the toilet. Becky goes to the bathroom in the middle of the night, sits on the toilet, and—boom—she doesn't know what's going on, falls right in the toilet! Can't get up! The suction is too much. She just can't lift herself up and out of the toilet. She says, "Abie, Abie, help me!"

Abie gets up and he starts pulling. Nothing's happening. Finally, she says, "You've gotta call the EMTs! You've gotta call the medics!" So he gets up and calls the medics.

Just as the medics are coming up the stairs, Becky realizes she's naked. She says, "Abie, Abie, what am I gonna do? I'm naked! They're going to see me naked!"

He says, "Here, take this yarmulke; put it between your legs." She does that.

The firemen come up, and they're banging, and they're pulling and yanking, and finally the chief fireman says, "We've got a problem."

Abie says, "What is it?"

So the fireman says, "Well, your wife's gonna be fine, but we couldn't save the rabbi."

HAROLD ZAPOLSKY

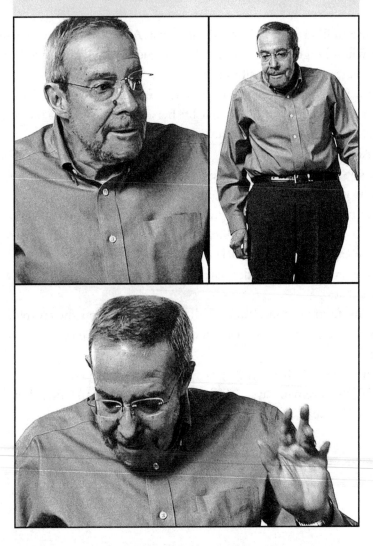

Harold Zapolsky's research interests are in theoretical physics, specifically in the areas of astrophysics and relativity. A good joke, according to Zapolsky, is either a slightly implausible tale, told with a straight face, about a perfectly plausible universe—or a plausible tale told about a slightly implausible universe. Either way, he notes, it is the sort of thing physicists do all the time.

Clock Shop

So this businessman is traveling through Europe, and his train stops in Zurich, Switzerland. And he knows that he's got three hours to make his next connection, so he figures he'll walk around the town a little bit.

He gets off the train and takes a look at his watch, and he sees that his watch has stopped, which is kind of awkward. So he thinks, Well, it's Switzerland, they've got to know about watches here. And he starts to walk around looking for a place, but it's a Sunday and all the shops seem to be closed.

Except, after about ten minutes, he sees this tiny little shop, and the window is completely filled with watches and clocks. And he says, "This is great. I wonder if he's open."

Checks the front door, the door is open, he walks in, and out of the rear of the store comes this elderly fellow wearing a yarmulke and a prayer shawl. Of course he's open on a Sunday; he's Jewish.

So the man says, "Look, I've got a terrible problem. I'm traveling through Europe. I have many meetings to make. I have many train connections to make. I'm going to stop in Geneva next and then Paris. And my watch has stopped on me, and I really can't function without the use of my watch. Can you please fix it?"

The man says, "Oh, I'm so sorry, I don't know a thing about watches. I'm a mohel. I perform ritual circumcisions."

And the man says, "Wait a minute, though. Your window is full of watches and clocks."

The man says, "Well, if you were in my profession, what would you put in the window?"

A Note About "Clock Shop"

I've heard this joke a number of times and, although the details change, one thing is consistent. The mohel or mohels always keep clocks in their window.

Why?

My first instinct was the similarity between the word *clocks* and the actual subject of a circumcision.

Here is Harry Zapolsky's theory:

I don't really think there is a connection. The businessman needs to have some item repaired to set up the joke—and what is more obvious than a watch—and that, of course, leads naturally to a shop with watches and clocks in the window.

This joke was first told to me by the wife of one of my grad school professors, at a student party sometime in the late fifties. At the time, it was considered to be highly risqué! *O tempore, O mores.* (Translation: "The times, they are a-changing.")

Zapolsky can think what he wants, but I'm sticking with my theory.

Lauren Johnson

Converting the Bear

A priest, a minister, and a rabbi want to see who's best at his job. So they each go into the woods, find a bear, and attempt to convert it. Later they get together.

The priest begins: "When I found the bear, I read to him from the catechism and sprinkled him with holy water. Next week is his First Communion."

"I found a bear by the stream," says the minister, "and preached God's holy word. The bear was so mesmerized that he let me baptize him."

They both look down at the rabbi, who is lying on a gurney in a body cast.

"Looking back," he says, "maybe I shouldn't have started with the circumcision."

ANNIE KORZEN

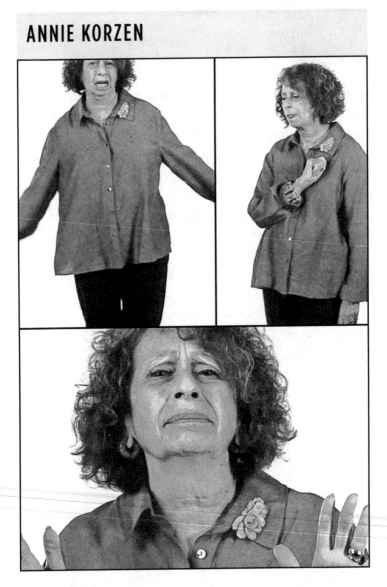

Annie Korzen is a writer and actress in Los Angeles. She has performed her solo show, *Yenta Unplugged,* on three continents.

Good Value

"Why are Jewish men circumcised?"

"Because no Jewish woman will touch anything that's not at least twenty percent off."

Mike Schwartz

(as told to him by his friend Haig Shekerjian)

The Ribbon Salesman

There was an old ribbon salesman named Goldberg who would regularly visit a buyer he found to be quite coarse and even anti-Semitic. For twenty years Goldberg would knock on the door of the buyer, and for twenty years he would leave, never making a sale.

One day, even before Goldberg could open his samples case, the buyer says, "Goldberg, tell ya what I'm going to do. I'll buy enough ribbon to reach from the tip of your nose to the tip of your penis."

Goldberg says, "Thank you very much," and leaves the office.

The next day Goldberg gets a frantic call from the buyer. "Goldberg, there are tractor-trailer loads of ribbon coming into my warehouse. What's going on?"

"You see," says Goldberg, "my nose is here, and the tip of my penis is in Poland!"

6

Food

What's in Our Mouths
While We're Talking

THIS PAST YOM KIPPUR MY DAD WAS FASTING AND SO WAS I. OUR thoughts inevitably turned to food. From where we were sitting, we could see a poster announcing the new Jewish calendar year of 5770.

My father turned to me and said, "It's amazing, the Jews have been around for five thousand, seven hundred and seventy years."

I nodded, weak from hunger.

He continued, "You know the Chinese just celebrated their year four thousand, seven hundred and seven?"

I smiled. Even in my debilitated state, I knew where he was going.

"That means the Jews had to go the first thousand years without Chinese food."

Of course, despite fondness for a Sunday night lo mein, the Jews have a rich culinary culture of their own. Granted, we're not the Italians, but we've got a few winners.

I recently took an informal poll, asking friends to name the quintessential Jewish food.

The responses:

- "Pastrami on rye."
- "Whitefish."
- "Potato pancakes . . . it was the only thing my Jewish mother-in-law would bring to my house . . . my kids ate them like cookies! And that's coming from a Catholic girl!"

- "Chocolate coins—the ones that come in the yellow net bag on Hanukkah."
- "Chopped liver—'cause we kvetch about how bad it is for you and then ask for more crackers."
- "Borscht and Mandel bread."
- "Chulent . . . among the Hasidic set."
- "Well, I'm not Jewish but I love apricot Hamentashen cookies."
- "Challah."
- "Noodle kugel."
- "Kreplach [dumplings]."
- "My father still eats gefilte fish every morning. Ick."
- "Nova on a bagel. Also lox."
- "Brisket—I think we all use the same recipe passed down from our great-great-grandmothers. Of course the sauce is actually from the back of a Heinz bottle but no Jewish grandmother in her right mind would admit that."

Personally, I vote for chicken soup with knaidelach, or as they are more commonly known, matzo balls. I always loved them as a child, despite the fact that some cruel cousin showed me a cartoon depicting the poor animal known as the "matzo"—he looked a little like a sad moose—who had to sacrifice his very own testicles for this ethnic soup.

In actuality, the balls, originally a Passover dish, are made of matzo meal (ground up matzo), eggs, oil, and water (or seltzer). They grow fluffy and round in a pot of boiling water and become a dense, delicious, sphere of, well, not-bread. They bob in the chicken soup, mingling with the little puddles of fat, the mushy carrots, and the limp stalks of dill—absorbing it all gently into their not-breadness.

Why do I believe the matzo ball is the quintessence of Jewish food?

Jews take great pride in divining rules from the scripture and then creating clever and ingenious ways to circumvent these rules. The matzo ball symbolizes that quality in the form of a meal. On Passover it is forbidden to eat bread or anything with flour. Except matzo. You can eat matzo because it hasn't risen and it's been rabbinically supervised. So we grind up the matzo until it's not-flour. Then we combine it with eggs and oil and make this delicious not-bread. Then we complete it by soaking it in the most nutritious broth on earth—the broth that has literally become cultural shorthand for nurturing.

It's clever, it's complicated, it's a little bit sneaky, and it's damn good for you.

FRED RUBIN

Fred Rubin says that words with a hard *c* or *k* sound are inherently funny. *Buick* is one of his favorites, especially as used in a particular scene in *Annie Hall*. He once wrote that "it'll be a sad day for comedy writers when General Motors goes under."

Bagel and Lox

Two old Jewish friends meet on the street. Max and Abe. Abe's got a grin on his face.

Max says, "What're you so happy about?"

He says, "I'll tell you what I'm so happy about. Down the block, I found a brothel, and—in this brothel, if you go in there—you pay fifty dollars, you ask for Gina, a gorgeous girl comes out. Huge breasts! She takes your penis, and she puts chocolate ice cream, nuts, syrup, whipped cream . . . and then she eats the whole thing off. It's fantastic!"

So his friend says, "Oh, I think I'll try that."

A couple of days later they meet on the street, and his friend is pissed as hell.

Abe says, "What's wrong with you?"

Max says, "I'll tell you what's wrong with me. I went to that brothel that you recommended."

He says, "Yeah, so?"

Max says, "I asked for Gina, I paid my fifty dollars, beautiful girl with big breasts . . ."

He says, "Yeah, so?"

Max says, "She takes my penis, she puts on cream cheese, a bagel, lox, onion, tomato . . ."

He says, "Yeah, so?"

Max says, "It looked so good, I ate it myself!"

RICKY COHEN

Ricky Cohen is a graduate of Princeton University and Yale Law School. At Princeton he played on the golf team. As a judge he sat on the Appellate Division of the New Jersey Superior Court. He is also an avid sailor.

The Chicken Case

Schwartz had a chicken farm and he had a longtime customer, Gottesman's Kosher Butchers. Gottesman had been a customer for years and they always did good business together but Schwartz noticed Gottesman was getting slow on his payments. When it got up to about eighty thousand dollars, Schwartz was upset about it and he spoke to Gottesman and said, "You gotta get me some money."

Gottesman promised him a ten-thousand-dollar check by the end of the month. The check never showed up. He promised him again; the check never showed up. So Schwartz went to his lawyers, McCarter & English, and told them to sue. They start suing. Gottesman files an answer. He says, "The chickens were no good, he didn't give me as many chickens as he was charging me for, the chickens wouldn't sell because they were so out of date, and anyway I don't know anybody named Schwartz, and I paid him."

Schwartz is angered by this reply and tells his lawyers, "We'll get him."

His lawyer says to him, "You know, Mr. Schwartz, we got a problem. You got a nice family business, but you got no records. You got no invoices, you got no sales records, you got no shipping records. You got nothing. We're gonna go to court and it's gonna be your word against Gottesman's."

"I don't care. The son of a gun is not playing fair with me. I'll take care of it. I'll send a chicken."

"You'll send who a chicken?"

"Judge Breitkof."

"You can't send Judge Breitkof a chicken. He'll be very insulted, he'll be outraged, he'll probably call the prosecutor, and you'll never win the case with stuff like that with Judge Breitkof. Don't do it."

"All right, no chicken."

They go to court, Schwartz testifies, Gottesman testifies, and at the end of the case Judge Breitkof says, "It would be an easier case to decide if there were records. But there are none, so I've had to judge the two men who appear before me and I find Schwartz to be a man of great character, complete credibility, Gottesman is obviously a dodgy character and not worthy of belief. Judgment for Schwartz: eighty thousand dollars."

As they're going down the steps of the courthouse, Schwartz says, "Great lawyers you are. You wanted me to settle; you wanted me to take less than I got. I took care of it."

"What do you mean you took care of it?"

"I sent him a chicken."

"You sent Breitkof a chicken?"

"Yeah."

"That was a terrible thing."

"Yeah, I sent him a note along with it."

"Oh my God—what did the note say?"

"It said, 'Judge Breitkof, enjoy the chicken and your family should enjoy it, too, and there's more where that came from if you know what I mean.'

"And I signed it, 'Gottesman.' "

A Note About Chicken Jokes

We shot the first round of these jokes in my home town of Highland Park, New Jersey. Several of the jokes—an inordinate amount, I thought—were about chickens. This made me curious.

It turns out that New Jersey was once a veritable hen-house of Jewish chicken farmers. At a time when rural land was inexpensive, many survivors of World War II started farms in the state and their prosperity peaked in the 1950s.

It was to be short-lived, however, as industrial farming and the increasing value of New Jersey real estate drove many of these farmers to either sell their land . . . or become real estate developers.

DIANE HOFFMAN

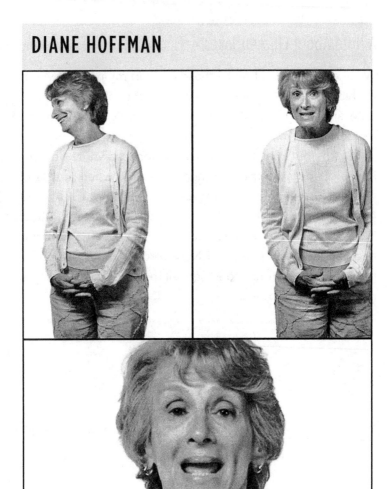

Diane Hoffman, my mother, was born in 1942 in Trenton, New Jersey. As I mentioned in the chapter "The Jewish Mother," she is one of those super-capable women of her generation who can basically do everything. She started a career in hospital administration later in life, after I was already off to college, and eventually ran the radiology department at St. Peter's, our local Jewish hospital.

Broccoli

A woman went into the greengrocer and asked the clerk for a pound of broccoli.

"Oh, ma'am, I'm so sorry. We just don't have any broccoli today. How about a pound of spinach?"

"Okay. I'll have a pound of broccoli."

"Maybe you didn't understand. We just don't have broccoli. How about a pound of string beans?"

"Um. All right. I'll have a pound of broccoli."

"Ma'am, we just don't have any broccoli. How about some asparagus?"

"No. I'll have a pound of broccoli."

Exasperated, he said to her, "Ma'am, can you spell *cat* as in *catastrophic?*"

"Of course. C-A-T."

"Can you spell *dog* as in *dogmatic?*"

Perplexed, she says, "Of course. D-O-G."

"Can you spell *fuck,* as in *broccoli?*"

"There's no *fuck* in *broccoli!*"

"That's what I was trying to tell you."

MIKE LEIDERMAN

Mike Leiderman describes himself as a patriotic son of the Catskills, having been "conceived in Liberty and raised in Monticello." Growing up, he snuck into every hotel nightclub he could when his parents took him to the mountains.

Last Meals

Three guys are going to be executed: a Frenchman, an Italian, and a Jew. They each get a chance to pick their last meal.

They ask the Italian, "What do you want?"

The Italian says, "Pasta primavera! I love-a pasta primavera!" So they bring him the pasta. He eats it, and they shoot him.

They say to the Frenchman, "What would you like?"

The Frenchman says, "Filet mignon." They bring him a huge filet mignon and he eats it. They shoot him.

They say to the Jew, "Well, what would you like?"

The Jew says, "Strawberries."

"Strawberries? We don't have any strawberries. They're out of season!"

The Jew goes, "Eh, I'll wait."

CHUCK BERKE

Chuck Berke grew up in Chicago, where he practiced law for several years. He then moved to Mexico to run a seventy-year-old health spa.

Rye Bread

Two elderly Jewish men are talking about their ailments. One of them says, "I haven't been with my wife sexually in many years. It's a part of my life that's behind me."

The other man says, "I have sex with my wife three or four times a week!"

He says, "Well, how do you manage that?"

The other man says, "Rye bread."

"Rye bread? Where do you get such rye bread? I've never heard of such a thing!"

He says, "There's a bakery at the corner. Just go in and get a rye bread."

The man goes in and he says, "I'll have a rye bread, please." Then he thinks, and he asks, "Well, how many loaves of rye bread do you have?"

She says, "We have five left."

He says, "I'll take all five loaves."

She says, "You know, by the time you get to the fifth, it'll be hard."

He says, "You know? Everyone knows!"

CHARLOTTE SPIEGELMAN

Charlotte Spiegelman is a psychotherapist based in Los Angeles. As far as we can tell, she is no relation to Eric. Or, if they are related, they certainly aren't close.

The Grasshopper

A grasshopper walks into a bar and orders a drink.

The bartender looks at him and says, "You know we have a drink here named after you?"

The grasshopper replies, "You have a drink named Stanley?"

JOE SIMONOWITZ

Joe Simonowitz was born in 1931. Before he retired, he was a salesman for Western Bagels.

Long Island Duck

A lady goes into a butcher shop in New York. She says to the butcher, "I want a Long Island duck."

He says okay, and brings out a duck. She sticks two fingers up the duck's tuches.

She says, "This is not a Long Island duck! This is a Florida fowl. Please, get me a Long Island duck!"

He goes in the back, and brings out another one. She proceeds to do the same thing. She says, "No! This is a Wisconsin chicken! If I want a chicken, I'll let you know. I want a Long Island duck!"

He goes in the back, brings out another duck. She does the same thing. She says, "Ah! This is a Long Island duck. Clean it, flick it, I'll wait for it."

As he's cleaning up the duck, she makes conversation.

She says, "What's your name?"

He says, "Irving."

She says, "Where you from?"

He turns around, drops his pants, and says, "I don't know—you tell me!"

7

Husbands and Wives

It's a Thin Line. . . .

BEFORE JEWISH COUPLES MARRY, THEY ARE REQUIRED TO SIGN A prenuptial contract of sorts known as a ketubah. The word *ketubah* is difficult to translate, but most scholars agree it means something to the effect of "here comes da pain."

A long-term marriage, in any faith, is a unique challenge. A couple needs to handle the pressures of raising a family, juggling careers and finances while still remaining intimate and interested in each other. It can't be easy. Of course, in my marriage, with my particular wife, who is almost certainly going to read this at some point—it's easy. I mean, couldn't be easier. It's easy like Sunday morning. But for most people, I would imagine, it's got to be tough.

Are we meant for monogamy? Does it really make sense to "mate for life"? Many animals do, including the gray wolf, the bald eagle, and the beaver. Can we learn any lessons from nature? Well, *gray wolf* and *bald eagle* could describe many older Jewish couples I know but clearly *beaver* has nothing to do with monogamy—so I guess that's a bust.

Long-term marriage obviously has its advantages. For men, these include never having to make another decision for the rest of your life; learning that your family, which you heretofore thought was fairly normal, is actually completely fucked up; and learning how to fail at being a mind reader. For women, it includes having a really big, hairy, smelly child to care for in addition to your children; learning how to field phone calls from the supermarket asking, "Which is the cereal that I like?"; and having a spare razor around to use on your legs.

But couples that survive find their balance. They scratch each other's itches and they provide something essential for each other. To an outsider they may seem like bickering old kooks who hate each other, but in fact they are bickering old kooks who hate each other who (really, actually) love each other.

SYLVIE DRAKE

Sylvie Drake joined the *Los Angeles Times* in 1971 and served as its chief theater critic from 1991 through 1993.

Report from the Doctor

Sam Mendelbaum comes home from work and finds his wife scantily dressed in front of the mirror, preening herself.

When she sees him, she says, "Oh, Sammy, I had the most wonderful report from Dr. Goldstein today. He said I had the body of a thirty-five-year-old, the face of a thirty-year-old, and the hair of a twenty-five-year-old."

And Sam says, "Yeah? What'd he say about your big, fat ass?"

"Sam, we didn't talk about you, darling, at all!"

MAX ROSENTHAL

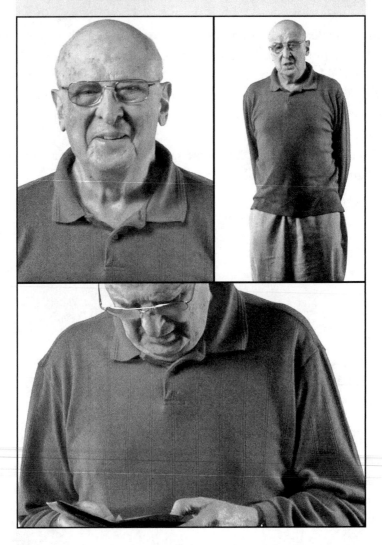

Max Rosenthal was born in Berlin and was forced to leave shortly after Kristallnacht. He and his family immigrated to the United States in 1939 and lived for many years in the Washington Heights section of Manhattan.

The Restaurant

These two couples get together at one of their houses, and afterward the husbands are talking in the living room; the women are in the kitchen. One of the men says, "I was at this restaurant yesterday. For twelve dollars, you can eat five meals—it's unbelievable! Fantastic! The food was delicious."

The other guy says, "What's the name of the restaurant?"

He says, "Uh . . . hmm . . . the name of the restaurant. I forgot the name of the restaurant. Oh, wait. What's that flower, that red flower? It smells good, it's got thorns on it . . ."

The other guy says, "You mean 'rose'?"

He says, "Yeah! That's it! Hey, Rose, what's the name of that restaurant?"

STEVE "SHECKY" PLATT

Steve Platt got a degree in agriculture from the University of Georgia and then enjoyed a wonderful career in the apparel industry.

Bank Robbery

During the commission of a bank robbery, one of the bank robbers' masks falls off. He puts it back on real fast. There are a couple of people standing off to his right, and he says to one of the guys, "When my mask fell down, did you get a look at my face?"

The guy says, "Yeah, I did."

He shoots him.

There's another guy standing next to the first guy, and he asks him, "When my mask fell down, did you get a look at my face?"

The second guy says, "Yeah, I did."

He shoots him.

There is a third guy standing there, and the bank robber asks him, "You know, when my mask fell down, did you get a look at my face?"

He says, "No, I didn't, but my wife did."

DENNIS SPIEGELMAN

Dennis Spiegelman has played poker with the same group of guys every Thursday night for the past thirty-six years. He refuses to disclose how much money he's lost over that time.

"I've Had Enough of Your Mother"

Frank and Lena are in their retirement home down in Florida. Frank calls his son and says, "Look, son, I've been married for forty-five years to your mother—I cannot take it anymore! I'm out of here! I can't take the kvetching and the criticism. I'm getting my own apartment. I'm leaving."

The son says, "Dad, don't do anything until I get back to you."

The son immediately calls his sister and says, "Look, sis, I just got this call from Dad. Mom and Dad are gonna get a divorce! We can't let this happen. We have to stop it. Why don't we go down to Florida and talk to them, and talk them out of it?" So, they agree.

He talks to his father and says, "Look, Dad, don't do anything rash. We're gonna come down. We're gonna talk to you—face to face—and show you the reasons not to get a divorce. When's the best time to come?"

He says, "Come on down on Friday."

"Okay, we'll see you on Friday."

Frank hangs up the phone, turns to his wife, and says, "Good news. The kids are coming for Passover and they're paying their own airfare."

IRA WOHL

Ira Wohl, born in 1944, is both a documentary filmmaker and a psychotherapist. His film *Best Boy* won the Academy Award for best feature documentary in 1980.

A Better Mousetrap

Max and Sadie are at home watching TV. She goes to the bathroom, and about a minute later he hears her screaming, "Max! Max! Come quick! It's terrible!"

He goes back to the bathroom and looks at her. She's sitting on the toilet. Her legs are spread apart, her support hose are down by her ankles, and she says, "It was terrible! A mouse came, he ran up my leg, and he went inside! What am I gonna do?"

He says, "I don't know! I don't know what to do! Just sit there, I'll call the doctor." So he goes to the phone and calls the doctor. The doctor says, "Look, just relax. Don't get nervous. It'll be okay. I can be there in twenty minutes but until I get there, go to the refrigerator and get a piece of cheese and see if maybe you can coax it out."

Max says, "Okay."

Twenty minutes later, the doctor comes up and walks back to the bathroom. He sees Max, lying across Sadie's thighs, waving a pickled herring back and forth.

He says, "What're you doing? I said 'cheese'!"

Max says, "I know, but I had to try and get the cat out first!"

SYLVIE DRAKE

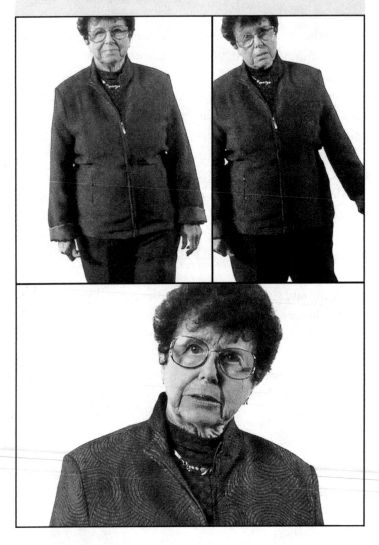

During the 1980s, Sylvie Drake was a personal interpreter for the playwright Eugene Ionesco.

"My Wife Is Poisoning Me"

This man goes to see his rabbi. He says to his rabbi, "Rabbi, I think my wife is poisoning me. I know she's poisoning me."

The rabbi says, "Calm down, calm down."

He says, "No, no, I know! But I don't know what to do. I need your advice."

The rabbi says, "Well, give me a chance to talk to her, and then I'll get back to you."

About three days later, the rabbi calls the guy, and he says, "I had a long talk with your wife. I talked to her for about three hours."

He says, "Yes, yes, so what's your advice?"

"Take the poison."

HARRY MACKLOWE

Harry Macklowe is a real estate developer based in New York City. In his words: "I grew up listening to my parents' generation of comedians, Jack Benny, Henny Youngman, Myron Cohen, instilling in me a lifelong appreciation of a well-told joke."

Kleptomaniac

A couple is in a supermarket. She has a problem, though. She steals; she's a kleptomaniac. She steals a can of fruit and is taken before the magistrate.

The magistrate says, "Sarah, how could you do something like that? What did you take?"

She says "Well, I just took one can of peaches."

"Peaches you took? How many peaches?"

"I think there were six peaches in the can."

"Sarah. You are going to go to jail for six nights. That's it, it's final."

"Oh my God."

Her husband stands up. "Your honor. She also stole a can of peas."

DANIEL OKRENT

Daniel Okrent's achievements in media and publishing are too numerous to mention. Seriously, too numerous. Also, an account of his writings (four books!) and scholarship (Shorenstein Fellow at Harvard's Kennedy School!) wouldn't fit in this space. But I would be egregiously remiss if I didn't tell you *he invented rotisserie baseball*! This is like having Thomas Edison tell you a joke.

Schmuck

Feldman comes down to breakfast one morning. He's sitting at the table having his breakfast. His wife's across the table as usual, with the newspaper in front of her.

She suddenly drops the newspaper, looks at him, and says, "I'm through with you."

He says, "What are you talking about? We've been married for forty years."

"Yeah. And for forty years you've been a schmuck. The day I met you you were a schmuck; I just didn't realize it. For forty years you've been the essence of schmuckness. You're such a schmuck, you're the second-biggest schmuck in the whole world."

Feldman says, "If I'm such a schmuck, how come I'm only the second-biggest schmuck in the world?"

"Because you're a schmuck."

NEIL ELLIOT

Neil Elliot was born in Manhattan, then lived in the Bronx, Queens (Laurelton), Denver, Portland, Burbank, and San Diego—all before college at Berkeley. After graduation, he managed a psychedelic rock nightclub in Hollywood from 1967 to 1969, moved back to New York to work in theater, and then moved back to Los Angeles, where he stayed.

A Divorce

Sadie and Moshe go to the divorce attorney. They've decided they want a divorce.

"Well, this is very hard," he says. "You've been married for sixty-three years!"

"That's right."

"And you're both in your eighties. Why do you want a divorce? Why now?"

"Well, we just wanted to wait until the children were dead."

MAX ROSENTHAL

Once Rosenthal finished school and ended a stint in the army, he studied pattern making and worked in the children's wear business for his entire career.

Flowers

These two ladies meet, and one of them says to the other, "Hi, how are you doing? I haven't seen you for a while. How's your husband?"

"Oh, my husband. He's such a wonderful man. He's such a doll. Every Shabbos, he brings home a bouquet of flowers for me."

She says, "Flowers? I hate flowers. Terrible. I can't stand flowers!"

"Why?"

"Because you know what I have to do when he comes home with flowers?"

"What?"

"You know . . . I have to lie down and spread my legs."

"Oh my! Don't you have a vase?"

STEVE "SHECKY" PLATT

Platt jokes that these days he is involved in "the table pad business" (those pads your grandmother used to put under the tablecloth). He says that the last time he got an order, "Truman was in the White House."

Traffic Stop

This elderly couple is driving in a car. She's driving; he's in the passenger seat. She has horrible, horrible hearing. They're on the freeway, and a police officer pulls them over. She rolls down the window.

The police officer says to her, "Did you know you were speeding?"

She turns to her husband and says, "What? What'd he say?"

Her husband says, "He wants to know if you knew you were speeding!"

The police officer says, "License and registration, please."

She turns to her husband and says, "What? What'd he say?"

He says, "He wants to see your license and registration!"

The police officer looks at it and says, "Oh, I see that you're from New Jersey. I dated a woman from New Jersey and, if I remember correctly, it was the worst sex I ever had in my life."

She turns to her husband and says, "What? What'd he say?"

Her husband says, "He says he knows you!"

Gershon Evan

Adam and Eve

After Adam was created, there he was in the Garden of Eden, all alone. Of course it wasn't good for him to be all by himself, so God came down to visit.

"Adam," He said, "I have a plan to make you much, much happier. I'm going to give you a companion, a helpmate for you—someone who will fulfill your every need and desire. Someone who will be faithful, loving and obedient. Someone who will make you feel wonderful every day of your life."

Adam was stunned. "That sounds incredible!"

"Well it is," God said. "But it doesn't come for free. In fact, this is someone so special that it's going to cost you an arm and a leg."

"That's a pretty high price to pay," said Adam. "What can I get for a rib?"

Cynthia Fisher

Bionic Penis

Mr. Goldberg wakes up in the hospital, bandaged from head to foot. The doctor comes in and says, "Ah, I see you've regained consciousness. Now, you probably won't remember, but you were in a pileup on the freeway. You're going to be okay, you'll walk again and everything, but . . . something happened. I'm trying to break this gently, but the fact is, your penis was chopped off in the wreck and we were unable to find it."

Goldberg groans, but the doctor goes on: "You've got nine thousand dollars in insurance compensation coming to you, and we have the technology to build you a new penis that will work as well as your old one did, maybe even better! But the thing is, it doesn't come cheap. It's a thousand dollars per inch."

Goldberg perks up!

"So," the doctor says, "it's for you to decide how many inches you want. But it's something you'd better discuss with your wife. I mean, if you had a five-inch one before, and you decide to go for nine inches, she might be a bit put out. But if you had a nine-inch one before, and you decide only to invest in five inches this time, she might be disappointed. So it's important that she plays a role in helping you make the decision." He agrees to talk with his wife.

The doctor comes back the next day and says, "So, have you spoken with your wife?"

"I have," says Mr. Goldberg.

"And has she helped you in making the decision?"

"Yes, she has," he says.

"And what is it?" asks the doctor.

"We're getting granite countertops."

8

Sex

What Is This I Hear About a Revolution?

SO THERE'S THE GARDEN, RIGHT? LET'S CALL IT EDEN.

There's a dude, Adam, and his lady friend, Eve, and everything is just perfect for, let's say, the first two chapters.

Then, in chapter 3, sex comes along and, like it always does, ruins the relationship.

Of course you know about Genesis chapter 3. Everybody, everywhere knows about chapter 3. Chapter 3 reads like a metaphoric reduction of a bad night out clubbing: The drug-dealing snake arrives, ecstasy apples are eaten, awareness of nakedness occurs, shame rains down hard, management gets super-pissed, everyone gets kicked out of the VIP room.

And the hangover—forever.

Oh yeah, and as an extra bonus, there's verse 16:

To the woman he said, "I will greatly increase your pains in childbearing; with pain you will give birth to children."

Thanks.

It doesn't take a semiotics professor to get the message here. The Old Testament puts it on a billboard early on the trip: Sex, despite that sweet burst of juicy apple flavor, is dirty, shameful, and bad. If you do it, God will know and he will be very disappointed. As in "I'm not angry, I'm just disappointed."

Cut to 1960. A little pill comes along called "the Pill." So much for verse 16. Suddenly biting the apple comes at a far more affordable cost. Women, and the men who want to love them, if only for a short while, grow braver. Emboldened by the tiny pill, they are willing to risk the approbation and disappointment of the Almighty. And you know what—they learn they can live with it.

For the Jews born in the 1930s and '40s, the sexual revolution spawned by the Pill arrived with their young adulthood. Some were already married with young children; many had grown up with parents who slept in separate beds. As *Playboy* grew in popularity and *Deep Throat* played at local theaters, the disappointed God of Genesis was still there in the back of their minds.

Conflict is the heart of the story and discomfort is the wellspring of humor. This sex-driven conflict and discomfort, between guilt and pleasure, between Genesis and the Pill, drives the humor of this chapter's jokes.

BARNETT HOFFMAN

Barnett Hoffman is a die-hard Rutgers Scarlet Knights fan. During their undefeated 1975–76 basketball season, our family traveled all over the eastern seaboard to follow their run to the Final Four. It doesn't get much better than that for a nine-year-old.

Fidelity

So Jake and Becky are married for fifty years, and it's their fiftieth wedding anniversary and Becky asks Jake, "Jake: all these years. All these years, have you been faithful to me?"

"Of course. Never have I strayed in fifty years. And you, Becky?"

"Well . . ."

"Becky. Did you hear me?"

"Yeah, I heard you."

"Well, you're not answering me."

"Well . . ."

"You mean to tell me?"

"Three times," she says.

"Three times! Tell me about it."

"The first time, you remember, Jake, you opened up that little dry goods store on Main Street. You had trouble getting that favorable lease because of that momzer landlord, and I went to go see the landlord. You got the favorable lease, didn't you, Jake?"

He says, "Well, you're right on that."

"The second time, Jake, remember, you were having financial difficulties, you wanted to get a loan at the bank and that no-good loan officer wouldn't lend you a nickel? You got your loan, didn't you, Jake?"

"Yeah, that's true. What was the third time?"

"Jake, do you remember a couple of years ago, you ran for president of the temple, and you were fifteen votes shy?"

ALMA PILLOT

Alma Pillot left home at age sixteen to dance on the nightclub circuit, working with the likes of Jackie Gleason and Lenny Bruce. After that, among many other things, she taught dance and served as a regional Hadassah president. At Hadassah, she put her talents to good use, staging fund-raising musical productions that starred enthusiastic temple members. Alma Pillot passed away on September 6, 2009.

Mom's Cooking

Mr. Rabinowitz hires a little girl to start working in his office and she's a beauty and he's got the hots for her.

And he tries to make time with her and she ignores him. One day he says, "Let me take you out to dinner. I'll take you to dinner; you have anything you want."

She says, "Okay."

So he takes her to this high-class restaurant, and they sit down and she orders a double lobster cocktail and a big bowl of soup and a gorgeous salad and a big steak with all the trimmings. Crêpe suzette for dessert. And orders a bottle of champagne.

And he's looking at her and he says, "Tell me, darling. Your mother cooks for you like this?"

She says, "My mother's not looking to fuck me."

MAX ROSENTHAL

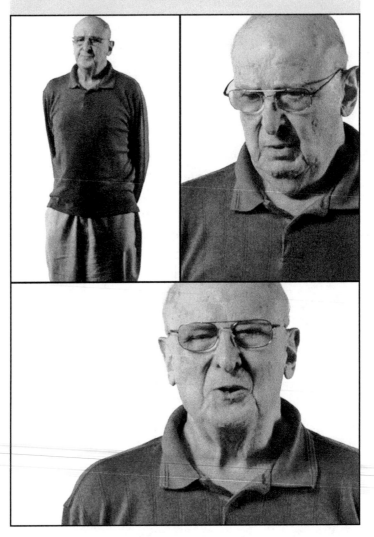

From Max's son Rich: "Whenever my brother and I would ask him what he wanted for his birthday, Hanukkah, anniversary, whatever, every time he would say the same thing. 'All I want are two nice boys.'

"That's Max."

The First Time

Mr. and Mrs. Shapiro go to the doctor and, at the end, the doctor calls in Mrs. Shapiro.

The doctor says to her, "Mrs. Shapiro, you're fine. You're husband's fine. There's just one problem: Your husband tells me that there's a little problem with his sex life. Just a little problem there."

She says, "So, what's the problem?"

"Well, he says, the first time it's perfectly fine. But the second time, he starts to perspire and sweat and is completely soaked afterward. You understand that?"

She says, "Yeah. The first time's in November; the second time's July."

MIKE LEIDERMAN

Mike Leiderman produces events and fund-raisers for a number of nonprofit organizations, including the Chicago Emmy Awards, the Fox Sports Net Awards for the March of Dimes, the NFL Players Association Mackey Award banquet for BBF Family Services in Lawndale (a section of Chicago), and the annual Jewish United Fund telethon.

Breakfast Lovin'

Abie and Becky are at the doctor's office. Abie says, "Doc, it's our sex life. It's terrible."

The doctor says, "Describe your technique."

Abie says, "Okay. Well, every Monday, Wednesday, and Friday . . ."

The doctor says, "Stop right there! That's the whole point. You can't plan these things. You must be spontaneous. Whenever the spirit moves you, that's when you have to act—with passion! Come back and see me in two weeks."

Two weeks later, they come back, and the doctor says, "How'd it go?"

Abie says, "Fan-tastic! You couldn't believe it! You're absolutely right! Spontaneity is the key! We were at breakfast. My wife dropped a spoon, bent over to pick it up, and—lo and behold—I got the urge like an animal! Right there on the breakfast table, three times we made love!"

The doctor says, "That's terrific. Any problems?"

Abie says, "Just one. They won't let us eat at Howard Johnson's anymore."

SIDNEY KIMMEL

Many people know that Sidney Kimmel is the founder and chairman of the Jones Apparel group, the producer of numerous acclaimed feature films, and a leading philanthropist—but who knew he could tell a joke?

Sexual Techniques

So these three old Jewish guys are bragging about their sexual exploits.

They had decided to compete and see who could make their wife moan and scream the most.

So the first guy says, "I win hands down. When I'm in the middle of having intercourse with my wife, I use a feather and she screams— she screams!"

Second guy says, "I can top that. I do it the Japanese style and in the middle of it, I use these marbles and it really works and she screams like crazy."

Third guy says, "I don't know what you guys are talking about."

He says, "I just jump on—do my one, two, six—and when I get off, I go over to the drapes, wipe myself off, and you should hear the *screams!*"

ANNIE KORZEN

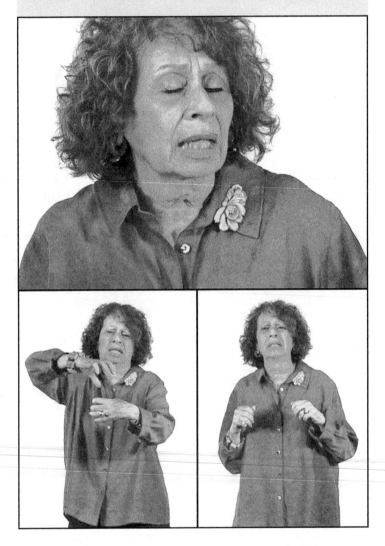

Korzen played the recurring character of Doris Klompus on *Seinfeld*, and John Turturro's mother in *Transformers: Revenge of the Fallen*.

Hello Dolly

This guy, Lenny, is having a one-night stand. In the middle of the night the lady says to him, "You know, this has been so much fun, I'm gonna let you in on a secret."

He says, "Really? What's that?"

"My vagina . . . can sing."

"You're kidding! Let's see!"

She pulls off the covers, he looks down, and he sees it singing, "Hellooo, Dolly! Well, hellooo, Dolly!"

Well, he's just astonished.

He says, "This is fantastic! You should go on the road! You should get bookings! We could make a lot of money off of this! I have a friend who's an agent. I'm going to call him right now." He calls his friend, the agent, Moe.

"Moe! It's Lenny."

"Whaddya want?"

"Moe, you won't believe this! I have this act! A singing vagina. You have got to listen to this! Listen to this!"

He puts the phone down between her legs.

"Hellooo, Dolly! Well, hellooo, Dolly!"

"You called me at three o'clock in the morning to hear some dumb cunt singing 'Hello, Dolly!'?"

MIKE MARCUS

Mike Marcus was a senior agent at the Creative Artists Agency during its heyday in the 1980s. His client list included Tom Cruise, Sydney Pollack, Robin Williams, Carl Reiner, Mel Brooks, John Landis, David Cronenberg, Roger Donaldson, Frank Oz, David Zucker, and Jerry Zucker.

"Hey, Kid!"

An old man is sitting on his rocking chair, rocking comfortably away. Over a hill, in front of his house, comes a young boy carrying something in his arms.

The old man says, "What've you got there?"

"Some chicken wire."

"What're you gonna do with that chicken wire?"

"I'm gonna catch me some chickens."

The old man says, "Oh, you danged fool! You can't catch no chickens with chicken wire!"

Of course, later that afternoon, up that hill comes that same kid dragging that chicken wire. There's a bunch of chickens stuck in it.

Next morning, the kid comes down the hill, carrying something in his hand.

"Hey, kid. What've you got there?" says the old man.

"I got me some duct tape."

"What're you gonna do with that duct tape?"

"I'm gonna catch me some ducks."

The old man says, "Oh, you danged fool! You can't catch no ducks with duct tape!"

Lo and behold, later that afternoon, that kid comes up the hill dragging a roll of duct tape. There's a bunch of ducks stuck to it.

Next morning, the kid comes down the hill, carrying something in his hand.

The old man says, "Hey, kid. What've you got there?"

"I got me some pussy willow."

The old man says, "Hang on! Lemme grab my hat!"

CHARLOTTE BORNSTEIN

Charlotte Bornstein grew up in Boston and later moved to Los Angeles. She still roots for the Sox and the Celtics and still cannot pronounce words with *r* in them.

Cab Ride

This woman in New York jumps into a cab, and she's stark naked. I mean, butt naked. She says, "Take me to Fifth and Broadway."

The cabdriver's looking in his mirror, and he's thinking, Oh, great. He says, "Lady, how do you plan on paying me? I mean, you have no clothes on, and you don't even have a purse with you—so how are you going to pay me?"

She says, "I'm gonna pay you with this," and points to her vagina.

He looks through the rearview mirror and says, "Lady, haven't you got anything a little smaller?"

RICHARD LEVINE

After my father retired from the bench he teamed up with a law firm to do mediation and arbitration. That's how we found Richard Levine. He is a longtime client of the firm.

Club Med

A woman meets her friend. She says, "How ya doin'? I understand you've been on vacation?"

She says, "Oy, what a vacation we had."

She says, "Where'd you go?"

"I went with Sarah and Sadie. We went to a travel agent, and she sends us to a place in the Caribbean called Club Med. We don't know from nothing. We go there, nice room, right on the beach, a pretty day. So we take our blanket, and we go sit on the beach. You won't believe what it was."

"What are you talking, 'what it was'? What was it?"

"It was a nude beach! People walking around naked. The men walking around hanging like this."

"No kidding?"

She says, "Yeah, then you know what happened?"

"What happened?"

"One of the men came over to the blanket. Sarah took one look and had a stroke."

She says, "Oh my God!"

"Then Sadie had a look and had a stroke!"

"You, Becky, are you all right?"

"Me?" she says. "I wouldn't touch that thing!"

MICHAEL BERGMAN

According to Mr. Bergman, his first full sentence was "A priest, a minister, and a rabbi walk into a brothel."

His intellectual development ended there.

Confession

An elderly, slight man walks into a church, walks over to the confessional, sits down. Priest pulls back the little curtain, the man doesn't say anything. He just sits there. Finally the priest, to move things along, says, "Can I help you, my son?"

The man says, "I vant you should listen to vat I'm going to tell you."

The priest says, "Okay . . ."

The man says, "Foist of all, you should know I'm eighty-seven years old."

"Eighty-seven. Has it been a good life?"

"Is ups and downs, good, bad, like everyting else, until eleven months ago."

"What happened eleven months ago?"

"My vife, Shirley, may she rest in peace, she pass avay."

"How long were you married?"

"Ve married sixty-three vonderful years. I vas so lonely, I don't know vat I would do, vat saved my life—there's a voman, a girl, maybe thirty-two years old, lives in the building, she comes over, she bring me a bowl of soup, a chicken . . ."

"What a Christian act!"

"Vell, ve never talked about nothing like that, but I vanted to say thank you, so at last I took her out to dinner to a nice place in the neighborhood, had a vonderful dinner, came back to the building, and she said that she had just made a fresh cake, you should come up and have a piece of cake, I go up to her apartment—to make a long story short, we ended up last night making love seven times."

The priest says, "Seven times?"

"That's right, seven times."

The priest says, "Can I ask you a question?"

"Ask me vatever you want to ask me."

"Are you Catholic?"

He says, "I'm not Catholic!"

"Then why are you telling me?"

"I'm telling everybody!"

HARRY RISKIN

Harry Riskin went to college with my father at Rutgers, where they were fraternity brothers. He has devoted his law practice to the area of real estate value litigation and the defense of property rights for property owners for over forty years. Riskin served as deputy attorney general for the state of New Jersey and was also special counsel to the commissioner of transportation.

The Towel

Murray is getting on in age, and he marries this much, much younger woman. As a result, they're having some problems with intimacy—the younger woman is just not being satisfied. So they decide to go see the rabbi for advice.

Murray tells the rabbi that he's trying to satisfy his young wife, and that he's been unable to do that. The rabbi strokes his beard thoughtfully and says to Murray, "Let's try something they did years ago. Go out and find a nice, handsome young man. Have him come in while you're making love and wave a towel while you're performing."

Murray and his wife agree to do what the rabbi suggests. They go out and find a handsome young man and they bring him into the bedroom with them. Murray gets into bed with his young, beautiful wife, and the young man waves a towel while they have sex. They try this a couple of times, and it doesn't work. The wife is getting no satisfaction. They decide to go back to see the rabbi again.

They tell the rabbi what happened, and the rabbi listens to them, and says, "Listen. Why don't you go back and try it again, but just reverse roles. Murray, you wave the towel. The handsome young man, he gets into bed with your wife, and let's see what that does. We do anything in the Jewish tradition to satisfy our wives."

They go home and go back into the bedroom. The handsome young man comes in, and Murray explains to him what has to be done. Murray picks up the towel, the handsome young man gets into bed with the wife, and they start having wild, passionate sex. The wife starts screaming, going absolutely crazy, having this wild orgasm.

Murray grabs the young man and says, "Schmuck, this is how you wave a towel!"

Mickey Antonetti

Two Surprises

One afternoon at the retirement home, Morris is talking to a fellow resident, Sadie, who he is interested in.

"So Sadie, you want to come to my room and do it?"

She agrees and they go to his room.

When they are finished, Morris says, "Sadie, if I knew you were still a virgin I would have done this long ago!"

Sadie replies to Morris, "And if I knew you could still get an erection I would have taken off my pantyhose."

A Bonus Freudian Knock-Knock Joke

"Knock knock."

"Who's there?"

"Cigar."

"Cigar who?"

"Penis."

9

Oral Sex

And Other Stuff That Probably Isn't Kosher

GROWING UP IN MY GENERATION, BEFORE THE INTERNET, SOME boys were introduced to oral sex through illicit copies of *Penthouse* or the stories of older friends or relatives. This joke (I can't recall the teller) was my introduction:

> *"How would you describe the worst blow job you've ever gotten?"*
> *"Terrific."*

Now that's something to anticipate!

Oral sex has long been taboo among all cultures. But for the Jews it has held a special concern, not because it is forbidden, but because it directly conflicts with two activities for which the mouth can more efficiently be used: eating and complaining.

In truth, Jewish men do have a commandment to reproduce. Consequently, during his wife's fertile period, theoretically, he shouldn't, shall we say, waste the seed. But outside of that commandment, the Halacha is fairly supportive of husbands and wives doing whatever they find mutually enjoyable.

"Honey, what do you mean you don't like to do it? The Halacha is very supportive of it. My birthday? That isn't for like eight months!"

I don't know, maybe the Halacha argument will work for you. If it does, let me know. Giving up bacon might be worth it.

ALLEN PINSKY

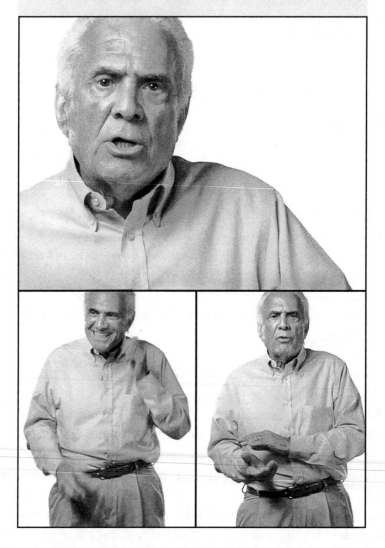

Allen Pinsky went to Camp Delwood with my dad. Then they lived in the same community in central New Jersey for many years, but my father never recognized him because he didn't have white hair when they were kids at summer camp.

Mr. Rabinowitz

Mr. Rabinowitz is suffering from a malady that nobody can diagnose. They've gone up to Mass. General, they've gone to Mount Sinai, University of California, University of Chicago, nobody can tell him what's happening. They finally go to a famous physician at Newark Beth Israel Medical Center.

The doctor says, "Mr. Rabinowitz. What's bothering you?"

He runs him through an exhaustive battery of tests and lo and behold, he discovers what's wrong.

"Mr. Rabinowitz, is your wife waiting for you?"

"Yes, she's in the waiting room."

"Will you step outside and ask her to come in here?"

She comes in and says, "Yes, doctor? What's the matter with my Irving?"

"Mr. Rabinowitz has a very, very rare disease. It's almost invariably fatal. There's only one cure for it."

"Yes, what's that? We'll do anything."

"The only thing that will help him is oral sex."

"What?"

"Oral sex. Do you know what that means?"

"Oh yeah, oral sex, I know."

She goes out and finds Mr. Rabinowitz in the waiting room.

He says, "What'd the doctor say?"

"You're gonna die."

BARNETT HOFFMAN

During my dad's tenure as a criminal judge, he started the Adult Substance Abuse Program, or ASAP. It's the only judicially supervised in-custody substance abuse program in the state of New Jersey and makes it possible for drug-dependent people to help themselves while incarcerated. I'm really proud of him for that.

Neil Armstrong

Some years ago, they were celebrating Neil Armstrong's landing on the moon. It was the thirtieth anniversary, and they said, "Mr. Armstrong, it's amazing—the feat that you did, and how you went down in history. Especially that wonderful quote: 'One small step for man, one giant leap for mankind.'"

And Neil Armstrong says, "I never said that."

"What are you talking about? Everybody knows you said that. It was all over the news! On television! It's recorded! It's taught in schools!"

He says, "That may be, but I never said that."

"Well, what did you say?"

"I said, 'One small step for man, one giant leap for Manny Klein.'"

A pause. "Really?"

"Yes."

"Well, where did that come from?"

And Neil Armstrong says, "When I was growing up in Brooklyn, our family lived next door to the Kleins—Manny Klein and his wife. The walls were very thin, and I used to hear Manny begging all the time that his wife should give him oral sex.

"And she would always say, 'Manny, when a man walks on the moon . . .'"

NORMAN STILES

Norman Stiles wrote and produced a television show, *Lomax, the Hound of Music,* for PBS. The hound dog hero is named Lomax as a tribute to Alan Lomax, the American folklorist and ethnomusicologist who traveled across America collecting and preserving American folk music. Alan Lomax is one of the inspirations for our website.

Paratrooper Training

Parachute training in Israel: Guy comes back from his first flight trying to make his first jump.

His friend says, "Well, how did it go?"

He says, "Oh, it was really scary. I was the last one 'cause I couldn't go first.

"So, I was last in line, and everybody was jumping and I'm getting seriously scared. And finally it's my turn and I'm holding on and I say, 'I can't do it, I can't jump, I can't.'

"And the sergeant barks at me, 'If you don't jump, I'm gonna fuck you up the ass.' "

His friend says, "Did you jump?"

He says, "A little at first."

HARRY MACKLOWE

You know that awesome Apple Store on Fifth Avenue at Fifty-ninth Street? The one with a glass cube entrance sitting on the plaza above? Putting the store there was Harry Macklowe's idea.

Sam and Becky

Sam and Becky are happily married for many, many years. They're approaching their fortieth anniversary, and every night they make passionate love.

Becky says to Sam, "You know something? You fill me with such enjoyment, but you always have the lights off. I'm going to turn the light on, for once."

And with that she reaches over and throws on the light switch. Then she looks down and sees Sam lying there, holding a vibrator.

Becky says, "My God! How can you explain that!"

Sam replies, "Darling, I can explain that if you can explain our two children."

JIM ROSENTHAL

According to Rosenthal, any fame and fortune that he finds by telling these jokes will go toward rebuilding Grossinger's, Brown's, and all of the Jewish Alps resorts.

Two Jewish Whales

There are these two Jewish whales, swimming in the ocean. One is Esther, and the other is Hymie. They're just swimming there, having a good time, and all of a sudden Hymie says to Esther, "Oy, I think we're in trouble."

Esther asks, "Why?"

"Well, see that ship down there? That ship is going to try to harpoon us."

Esther says, "Harpoon us! What is a 'harpoon'?"

Hymie says, "Well, it's like a big bow and arrow."

"Oy, Hymie, what are we going to do?"

"Well," he says, "we have to swim over there, and through our blowholes blow very hard and turn the ship over and drown all the sailors."

"Oh, okay."

So they swim out to the ship, they do the blowing, the sailors go over, and Esther says, "So, Hymie how did I do?"

"Oh, you did terrific, but we still got trouble."

"What's the matter?"

"Well, you see that other ship over there? That ship is going to come here, save all the sailors, and then they're going to try to harpoon us again."

"Oy," says Esther. "What do we have to do?"

"We have to go there and eat all of those sailors."

Esther thinks for a minute, and says, "Hymie, you talked me into that blow job but I'm not swallowing the seamen."

LOUISE YOHALEM

Louise Yohalem, the mother of my dear friend Eve, is a cabinet-level college administrator and an expert and educator in human sexuality. She has devoted a tremendous amount of time and energy to educating young people about prevention of pregnancy and sexually transmitted diseases. This includes a stint on the New Jersey governor's Advisory Committee on Adolescent Pregnancy and nine years as the executive director of development at Union County College.

Sex Therapist

The Shwartzes have been married for many years and they hear about this therapist who does amazing things for people who have been married for a long time. What the heck have they got to lose? They'll see the therapist.

They get to the therapist's office, and she says, "I have a very unusual way of working. I'm going to take each of you separately into my examining room and I'm going to examine you. If I feel we can work together, then we'll proceed and if I feel there's nothing in my techniques to help you, well, there'll be no charge for the session."

So she takes them each separately into the examining room and she brings them together and she says, "I think we can do great things together."

So they have their session and at the end of the session she says, "I have some homework for you. On your way home I want you to stop at a supermarket. You, sir, buy a bunch of grapes. And when you get home, your wife will disrobe and you'll take the grapes and lay them on the bed, in a line between her legs all the way up to the opening of her vagina. You, madam, buy a doughnut. And when you get home and your husband's member is erect, place the doughnut on your husband's erect member and eat your way all the way around it."

Well, it sounds very strange, but what have they got to lose, they've paid this person. They go home, they do what she said, and it's just amazing what it's done for their marriage. And they're so happy they tell all their friends about it.

So one night the Cohens say, "You know, the Schwartzes have had such an extraordinary experience. We're married a long time, why don't we go and see this therapist?"

So the Cohens go to see the therapist and the therapist says, "I have a very unusual way of working. I'm going to take each of you separately into my examining room and I'm going to examine you. If I feel we can work together, then we'll proceed and if I feel there's nothing in my techniques to help you, well, there'll be no charge for the session."

So she sees them both separately and she brings them back together and she says, "I'm very sorry, I don't think this will work. There'll be no charge."

The Cohens say, "What do you mean you won't work with us? The Schwartzes raved so about you. You have to work with us!"

She says, "Look, I really don't think that my methodology is right for you."

"Please! Please!" say the Cohens. "We'll pay you! We won't hold you responsible."

The therapist shrugs and says, "Okay."

They have a session and at the end of the session she says, "I have homework for you. On the way home I'd like you to stop at a market. You, sir, buy an apple. You, madam, buy a box of Cheerios."

Daniel Elias

Cowboy Boots

Murray was in a rut.

So he decided to do something different. He went out and bought some cowboy boots.

He went home and said, "Sadie, do you notice anything different?"

Sadie says, "Vat difrnt? Same shirt. Same hair. Same punim. Same Murray."

So Murray runs to the bedroom and takes off everything excepting his new cowboy boots and comes out and says, "So now do you notice anything new?"

"Vat new—it's still pointing down!"

Murray replies, "It's pointing on mine new cowboy boots."

Sadie responds, "You should have bought a hat!"

JAY ORLIKOFF

Jay Orlikoff practiced family and cosmetic dentistry on Long Island for thirty years before retiring in 2002. On the evening of May 1, 1998, he was honored by the New York State Academy of General Dentistry with the Meritorious Service Award.

A Flea Goes on Vacation

A flea goes to a travel agent and says, "I've worked really hard. I'd like to take a vacation."

The travel agent says, "Where would you like to go?"

"I have no real preference. Just someplace nice and warm."

So the travel agent looks in different books and he says, "I've got just the place for you. I can book seven days in Ringo Starr's hair. Ringo Starr is in Nice, France. It's nice and warm; you should have a great time."

So the flea says, "Okay."

Four days later, the flea comes back to the travel agent. The travel agent says, "What's the matter?"

"That was terrible. Ringo Starr stays in his room all the time, plays the drums, I got a headache. It was terrible."

"Well, let's see. We can book seven days for you in Omar Sharif's mustache. Omar Sharif's gonna be in Monte Carlo; you'll have a great time there."

The flea says, "Great." He goes there. Four days later, he's back. Travel agent says, "What's the matter?"

"Omar Sharif, he plays bridge all the time, he's in the casino. I never saw sunlight, it was a horrible vacation."

"Man, you're difficult. Let's see what we can do for you."

He looks and he says, "This one you'll love. I can book seven days for you in Brigitte Bardot's muff."

"Brigitte Bardot's muff, that sounds great. Where's she gonna be?"

"St.-Tropez. Nice and warm, sunny."

"I'll go."

Four days later, the flea's back. The travel agent says, "I don't believe it. What happened?"

"Well, every day she was out in the sun by the pool. She was listening to great music. People were waiting on us hand and foot."

"What was wrong?"

"Four days later, I was in Omar Sharif's mustache again."

A Note About "A Flea Goes on Vacation"

One of the fun things about these jokes is trying to determine when they were first conceived.

This joke, at least in the form told by Dr. Orlikoff, has some very strong clues. The cast of characters includes Omar Sharif, Brigitte Bardot, and Ringo Starr.

Between 1962 and 1968, Sharif was huge—starring in *Lawrence of Arabia, Doctor Zhivago,* and *Funny Girl.* This period coincides with the heyday of Bardot's career and almost the entire existence of the Beatles.

If this joke were a bottle of red wine, it might be worth quite a bit by now.

Gaynor Cote

(retelling a favorite joke of the late Marcia Tucker,
who was the founding director of New York City's
New Museum of Contemporary Art)

Seventeen Pigeons

Sadie and Bessie and Rose are bragging about their husbands at the club.

Sadie says, "My Herman, he loves me so much he bought me this ten-carat diamond ring."

Bessie says, "Hah, my Irving, he adores me, just look at this beautiful full-length mink coat."

Rose says, "Well, my Bernie, he loves me and he has a schlong so long that seventeen pigeons can stand on top of it side by side."

The other two women sit stunned and silent for a couple of minutes, then Sadie says, "Ah, I can't lie. The diamond, it has a big flaw. See, right there."

Bessie sighs and says, "Since we are telling the truth, I gotta tell you, the coat, it's used and there a little rip in the lining. Look here."

Rose responds, "All right already. The last pigeon, number seventeen? His left foot, it slips a little."

Jim Rosenthal

Car Troubles

There's a penguin who is driving his car home. All of a sudden, the car starts to act up. So he pulls into a garage and he tells the mechanic, "It's not operating."

The mechanic says, "I'll have to have an hour at least to diagnose the problem."

So the penguin goes into town to kill some time. He sees a walrus and some sea lions. As he's coming back to the garage he sees an ice cream parlor run by a polar bear. He stops and buys a vanilla ice cream. While he's walking back, because of his short little arms, he drops a big glop of the ice cream on his foot.

When he gets to the garage, the mechanic sees him and says, "You blew a seal!"

The penguin looks down at his foot and says, "No! That's ice cream, that's ice cream!"

10

Illness and Doctors

I'm Not Sure Which Are Worse

THE WONDERFUL THING ABOUT MODERN MEDICINE, FEW WOULD argue, is that it allows us a longer life and therefore more time to complain about doctors.

Jews have a complicated relationship with doctors. Most of us had mothers who wanted us to be doctors, so it's natural that we hate the people who lived up to our mother's expectations when we, obviously, did not.

On the plus side, doctors are required by their profession to listen, pay attention, and nod their heads thoughtfully when we kvetch—so, in that respect, we find them very useful.

In my exhaustive research (Wikipedia) I have found no solid evidence that the Jews invented hypochondria, but there is some evidence that we are quite good at it, maybe even in the top two. In her book *Hypochondria: Woeful Imaginings,* Susan Baur writes that "many doctors get the impression that hypochondria is more prevalent among Jews and Italians. Regardless of absolute numbers, illness and fear of illness among members of these groups is more openly expressed."

Baur's point is that among the Jews and our Mediterranean cousins the Italians, it's the comfort in expressing—as opposed to *repressing*—feelings, pain, and anxiety that leads to hypochondria.

I'll buy that. It doesn't take a giant leap to suggest that the jokes in this chapter are a way of expressing the fear and anxiety associated with illnesses and the people who try to treat them.

BERT BUSCH

Bert Busch's mother, Jeanette, was the second of my grandfather's five sisters. His brothers Malcolm and Ron also contributed jokes. When we were growing up in the seventies, Bert had a groovy mustache that made him look a little like Gomez from the Addams Family.

Health Care

A doctor is showing a female benefactor around the hospital.

And as they look into one of the patient rooms, they both, to the horror of the female benefactor, see this male patient furiously masturbating.

And the woman says to the doctor, "Oh my God. What's going on there?"

And the doctor says, "Madam, I'm terribly sorry you were exposed to this. This patient has a terrible health condition. If he doesn't masturbate at least five times a day, his testicles fill up with semen, they could rupture, and he would be terribly sick."

And the woman says, "Oh, in that case, well I guess I understand."

They're walking past the next room and there is another male patient, and a female nurse is performing oral sex on him.

And with that, the woman says, "How can that be justified?"

And the doctor says, "Same condition. Better health-care plan."

EILEEN LOTTMAN

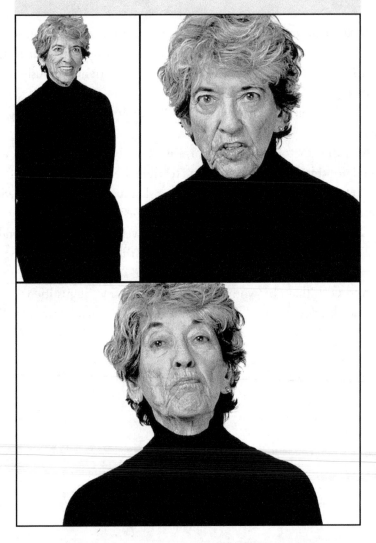

Eileen Lottman has written and published twenty-three novels and has been working on the twenty-fourth for the past eighteen years.

Test Results

Mrs. Green calls the doctor's office and she says, "My husband, David Green, had some tests the other day and I'm calling to get the results."

The nurse says, "Well, we have two David Greens in this practice and they both had tests and I just got the lab results and one of them has AIDS and one of them has Alzheimer's."

Mrs. Green says, "Oh. Well, how am I gonna tell? How do I know which one he has?"

The nurse says, "Well, I suggest that you send him to the store to buy bread. And if he finds his way home, don't fuck him."

JOHN PLESHETTE

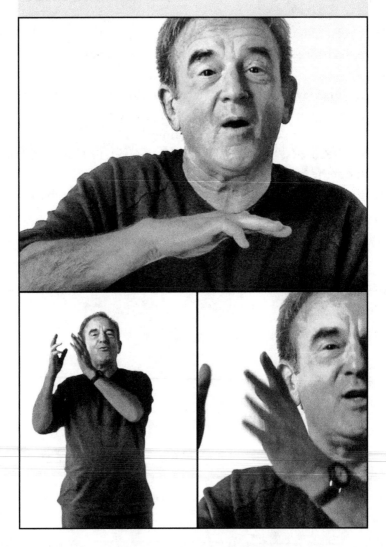

John Pleshette is an actor, writer, and director. His longest-running acting role was as Richard Avery on *Knots Landing,* which he played for eight years. He considers himself a New Yorker, although he has lived for thirty-five years in Los Angeles, where he struggles on a daily basis to retain his sense of humor.

Doctor's Advice

A guy goes to his doctor. The doctor says, "Look, I don't know how to tell you this, but you've just got to stop masturbating!"

The guy says, "Why?"

The doctor says, "So I can examine you!"

MALCOLM BUSCH

Malcolm Busch is a first cousin of my father's. "Dr. Drobkin" is an outstanding example of a story that is well practiced and honed to perfection. I especially love his use of the word *stripling*. Right now, I laughed a little just typing that word.

Stripling.

Dr. Drobkin

Dr. Drobkin is a very world-famous specialist in a highly specialized field of cardiology. He got his undergraduate degree, his medical degree, and his Ph.D. in his hometown, then practiced as a research doctor at the highest level in New York. He wrote a significant paper and he's been invited to deliver the paper at a meeting, which, by coincidence, is in his hometown.

The room is full of men and women, the men wearing tuxedos, the women properly attired for such an august event. Dr. Drobkin approaches the dais, puts his notes on the lectern as he's about to give the talk, and suddenly the papers all slide to the floor.

He bends over to pick them up, and as he does, his tuches is against the microphone, and at the very wrong moment, lets one ride that reverberates throughout the room, magnified by the microphone. Somehow he gains his composure and delivers his paper. No sooner than he's done, he grabs everything up and makes a quick exit through the rear door. And never comes back to the town again.

Well, many years pass, his mother is on in years, and he has to go back to town to care for his mother. He does so under the name of Dr. Cohn, makes a reservation at the local Hyatt under that name, gets there under cover of darkness, checks into the hotel.

A bright-eyed and bushy-tailed room clerk says, "Oh, good evening, Dr. Cohn. Have you ever been in our town before?"

The doctor says, "As a matter of fact, young man, I grew up here, I got my education here, got my doctorate here at the university, and I moved away."

The young man says, "Oh, why haven't you been here, sir?"

"Well, a number of years ago, a very embarrassing thing happened here and I just didn't feel that I could come back and face the people in the town."

"Doctor, far be it from me, a young stripling, to advise a distinguished older gentleman such as you, but if I can give you anything from my experience and my young life, things that I thought were embarrassing and people noticed, I later found out that no one even knew that they happened. I'm sure that's probably true of the thing you think is so embarrassing."

"No, I doubt that anyone has forgotten this."

"Well, was it a long time ago?"

"Yes, it was a very long time ago."

The young man says, "Was it before the Drobkin fart or after?"

A Note About the Drobkin Joke

Sent to the Old Jews Telling Jokes website by L. Weinman:

You may, or may not, be interested in knowing that the "Drobkin" joke has a *looooong* history.

As told on your site it is almost identical to a story in *A Thousand and One Nights,* which I believe was written down about the year 1200.

In that version Abu-Hassan is a very wealthy merchant, and one night holds a grand dinner for the caliph and many men of importance.

During the dinner he breaks wind "loud and terrible." Feigning a call of nature, he runs away.

There are at least, by memory, about one hundred pages that describe his travels and adventures over the next ten years.

He finally decides that it may be time for him to come back home, but he wants to check things out.

He, by this time, does not appear to be the same man who left—age and adventures—and he wanders around the town without hearing anything bad.

On his way to his house, he passes a woman and her daughter sitting/working in front of their house.

The daughter asks the mother, "When was I born?" and of course, the mother answers, "Thou wert born on the night Abu-Hassan farted."

RONNIE BUSCH

Ronnie Busch is the third Busch brother to tell a joke on the site. He has always been remarkably fast with a one-liner. When I decided, after college, to forgo law school and go into the movie business, he quipped, "Great! Rin Tin Tin needs a stand-in." It turned out not to be true. Rin Tin Tin has this little bitch he's been working with for years.

Emissions

Mr. Ginsberg is a resident of Rossmore. He's ready to go to Florida for the winter and he goes in to see Dr. Schwartz, an internist.

The doctor says, "What's the problem?"

He says, "Well, I've been having these silent gas emissions, and I just don't know what to do about it, and it's causing a lot of problems and a lot of embarrassment."

"Well, tell me about it."

"The other night we were playing bridge; my wife and I were at the Grossmans'. And during the course of the evening I probably had six or eight of these silent gas emissions. It created a little bit of a noxious odor, but they were all silent so there were really no problems.

"We went home and it happened again the other night at dinner so I decided to come see you. As a matter of fact, I've had eight or ten of these incidents as I sit here today. What can you do for me, Doctor?"

The doctor says, "Well, the first thing I'll do for you is send you to a hearing specialist."

CHARLOTTE BORNSTEIN

When Charlotte Bornstein began the Charlotte-James skin-care company in Los Angeles thirty years ago, she fulfilled a lifelong ambition to "be in the skin business."

Dwarf and Shrink

A very small man walks into a psychiatrist's office. He says to the psychiatrist, "By any chance, do you treat dwarves?"

He says, "Yes, I do. You'll just have to be a little patient."

A Bonus Joke from Charlotte Bornstein

Invisible Man

A guy walks into a psychiatrist's office and says to the secretary, "I need to see the psychiatrist, immediately."

The secretary says, "What seems to be the problem?"

He says, "Well, I think I'm invisible."

So the secretary knocks on the door of the psychiatrist's office, walks in, and says, "Dr. Smith, there's a man in the waiting room who claims to be invisible."

The doctor says, "Tell him I can't see him."

LARRY ZICKLIN

Larry Zicklin endowed the Zicklin School of Business at Baruch College. He also endowed the Carol and Lawrence Zicklin Center for Business Ethics Research, at the University of Pennsylvania's Wharton School of Business.

Everything Hurts

A redheaded lady, beautiful lady, walks into the doctor's office and says, "Doctor, you've gotta help me. I'm in terrible pain. Everything in my body hurts. Not one thing, but everything."

Doctor says, "Everything?"

"Absolutely everything."

Doctor says, "Show me."

She says, "Well, look. [Presses head.] Oh! I'm in terrible pain when I do that. [Presses neck.] Oh, and that's worse!"

She touches her side, and then she starts to scream. She touches her leg; she's in anguish.

Doctor looks at her and says, "You're not a redhead, are you?"

She says, "Well, not really."

He says, "You're a blonde."

She says, "I am. How did you know?"

He says, "Your finger's broken."

BARNETT HOFFMAN

My dad was the only one of the first season's joke tellers to come back for season two. Initially I wasn't sure if it was a good idea. But he sat me down and patiently explained that if I didn't let him tell a few more jokes, I wouldn't be allowed to go to the prom. This is probably good, as I have no idea where I put my gray Capezio jazz shoes.

"I Must"

A Frenchman, a German, and a Jew are walking through the desert and it's so hot in this desert.

They're schlepping along and trudging, and the Frenchman says, "I am so tired. I am so thirsty and tired. I must, I must have some French wine."

They're trudging along and the German says, "I am hot. And I am tired. I must, I must have some good German beer."

They walk a little farther and the Jewish guy says, "Oy am I tired. Am I tired, am I tirsty. I must. I must.

"I must have diabetes."

Herman Koltnow

Tea Leaves

Becky woke up one morning with a tormenting rectal itch. She had never experienced anything as terrible. She thought she could suffer in silence, but as it became more severe she had to seek help.

She told her neighbor Sadie. Sadie said, "I know just what to do. When you have your tea, take the leaves from the pot and apply them to the itch. You'll feel better in no time."

Becky did as she was told, applying her tea leaves to the area. She had a few hours of relief, but later in the day the itch was back, worse than ever.

In despair she decided to consult Sammy Schwartz, the local quack.

"Sammy," said Becky, "I've got a problem: a tormenting rectal itch."

Sammy looked pensive and said, "Becky, get on the examining table and I'll see what it looks like."

Becky positioned herself on the doctor's table and Sammy, in his best professional manner, went to investigate.

"Oy!" cried Sammy in shock.

"What is it?" Becky asked frantically.

"You're going to meet a tall stranger and take a long voyage."

11

Getting Old

Florida, as in Southeast, and Surgery, as in Plastic

"Doctor, I can't pee."

"How old are you?

"Ninety."

"You've peed enough!"

It would certainly be Hebocentric to claim that the Jews have suffered the effects of aging and the march of time more than any other ethnic group (although it could probably be argued that the Jews have probably kvetched more about it!).

Through two groundbreaking discoveries, however, the American Jew has probably had more success than any other group in history of reversing or at least mitigating the unpleasant side effects of a long life. The American Jews did not invent either of these remedies, and we certainly do not lay claim to using them exclusively, but we have been strong proponents and advocates of both. These are: Florida, as in southeastern, and surgery, as in plastic.

Ponce de Leon explored Florida in the 1500s looking for the "fountain of youth" and the American Jews pretty much found it at the Miami Fontainebleau, starting in the late 1950s. With the success that followed the war years, American Jews were able to do something that their forebears had never done: retire. While they still wanted to spend the summer months up north with their perfect grandchildren, what was wrong with having a little sunshine during the dreary winter? Jewish communities developed in Miami Beach, Hollywood, Boca Raton, and for the fancy-shmancies, Palm Beach.

While Florida couldn't actually stop the aging process, it could certainly slow it down. How slow? About twelve miles per hour if you've ever taken a drive around early-bird-special dinnertime. Retired Jews were able to stay active and fit doing all the things they liked the most: playing golf, practicing bridge, lobbing a tennis ball back and forth, betting nickels at mah-jongg, and, especially, complaining that their children don't call enough.

The Jews certainly did not invent plastic surgery. Apparently the Indians were performing it as early as a thousand years ago. Whatever. The Chinese invented spaghetti but you wouldn't ask for a Bolognese in Beijing. Plastic surgery is endemic to all contemporary American life, and isn't limited to any particular ethnic group, but the Jews, as is their wont, have put their own spin on it.

When elective cosmetic surgery starting becoming possible and popular in the 1960s, the Jews were in a quandary. They liked the idea of a little nip and tuck but didn't know whether it was, well, kosher. So a number of major rabbis were asked to opine on the subject.

Quoting various sources in the Halacha, most of the rabbis came to the same opinion: It was allowable to do the plastic surgery if one was preventing shame and suffering by correcting a defect in one's looks. It was forbidden if the cause was vanity alone. And there the rabbis managed to completely satisfy their constituency. Not only did they give the Jews backdoor permission to have plastic surgery, but they gave them a good reason to find themselves defective!

DANIEL OKRENT

Daniel Okrent, like Isaac Newton and that guy Murphy, has a "law" named for him. Okrent's law: The pursuit of balance can create imbalance because sometimes something is true.

Three Old Jews

So these three old Jews are sitting on a traffic island on Broadway as they do on most sunny mornings.

One of them says out of nowhere, "Ech. It's terrible. I hate it. I just can't stand it."

The other one says, "Max, what's wrong with you?"

Max says, "It's being eighty-five years old. You know, every morning I get up, it's seven o'clock, I go to pee. I stand there, I push, I squeeze, nothing comes out—a little dribble, dribble, dribble if I'm lucky. It's terrible."

His friend says, "I know what you mean."

"Why? What's your problem?"

"Every morning, you know, I try to move mine bowels. I push, I sqeeze, I grunt, I groan—maybe raisins if I'm lucky. It's terrible."

The third guy says, "I know what you mean. Being old, it's just awful."

Max says, "What's your problem, Sol?"

He says "Well, every morning, seven o'clock, I pee like a golden fountain. Eight o'clock, I have a nice bowel movement. Nice juicy plums."

"What's wrong with that?"

He says, "I don't get out of bed until nine."

EILEEN LOTTMAN

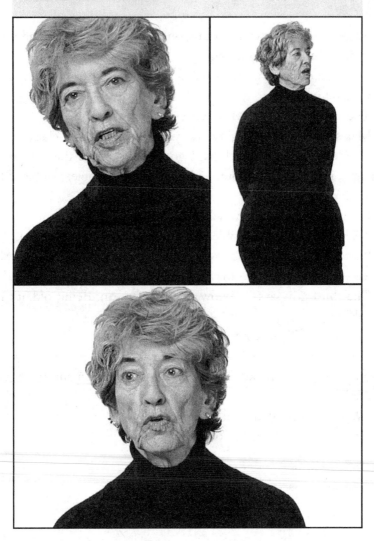

Eileen was married for forty-five years to the late Evan Lottman. She refers to him as the "best motion picture film editor in the business" and, although she would be the first to acknowledge bias, she may be right. Among many other films, Evan edited *Sophie's Choice, Panic in Needle Park,* and parts of *The Hustler* and *Apocalypse Now,* and was nominated for an Academy Award for *The Exorcist.*

Super Sex

A little old lady in the nursing home goes up to the last remaining man in the nursing home.

She gets herself all dolled up and says, "How would you like some super sex?"

He says, "I'll take the soup."

Irwin Ira Steinberg

Blame the Dog

Avi's wife passed away a few years back and he's decided that he will finally go on a date. His neighbor Atle, a widow herself, has invited him over. They are sitting in the living room chatting, with her dog resting on the floor near Avi. As this is his first date since his marriage, he is very nervous and has developed a terrible case of flatulence and can't control himself. He lets one rip.

"Spot, get away," Atle says, but the dog doesn't move.

Avi thinks to himself, Wow, she is so nice that she is pretending this is the dog's fault—my late wife would have never done such a thing.

He then lets another one out, even louder than the first.

"Go away, Spot," she says, even louder.

This is incredible, Avi thinks. What a considerate woman! And of course he lets one more go.

"Get out, Spot!" Atle yells. "Before he craps all over you!"

HARRY RISKIN

Harry Riskin was selected as a "New Jersey Super Lawyer" by *New Jersey Monthly* magazine.

The Breakfast Table

Becky and Jake have been married for fifty years and they're at the breakfast table.

Becky says to Jake, "Can you imagine, we've been at this breakfast table for fifty years and it's just been wonderful being with you."

And Jake says, "Yes, I can remember. As a matter of fact, I can remember sitting here naked as a jaybird with you at this very breakfast table."

So Becky says to him, "You know what? Let's relive old times, Jake. Let's get nude."

So they strip and they get right down to the buff and they come back to the table and sit down.

Becky says, "Jake, my honey. You know my nipples are as hot for you today as they were fifty years ago."

Jake says, "That doesn't surprise me. One's in the coffee and the other's in the oatmeal."

RICHARD CHESNOFF

Richard Z. Chesnoff, in his role as a global correspondent, had the opportunity to interview Yasser Arafat many times. "Once in the late eighties at his headquarters in Tunisia," Chesnoff says, "Arafat invited me to stay on for lunch. The table was filled with familiar Palestinian delights—hummus, tahini, parsley and bulgar salad, pita, etc. There was also a huge tureen in the middle of the table filled with liquid with what looked like floating chunks of meat and vegetables. I asked what it was. 'Chicken soup,' Arafat said! 'It's my favorite and I have it every day.' I laughed and told him he had more in common with Yitzhak Rabin, Israelis, and Jews than he thought. 'We call it Jewish penicillin,' I told him. I'm not sure he got it, and after he offered me a chicken leg with his fingers, I decided I'd rather not try it."

Morris Turning Ninety-five

Morris is about to turn ninety-five. His sons want to give him a birthday present but they don't know what to get him. They talk back and forth—maybe we'll give him this, maybe we'll give him that.

They go to visit Morris in his nursing home. "Papa," they say, "it's going to be your ninety-fifth birthday. What would you like as a present?"

Papa says, "Well, fellahs, I'm getting a little lonely here. Maybe you'll bring me a nice young woman, put her in my bed with me, and I'll have an afternoon with her?"

The boys are shocked! They talk to one another—we can't do that, it's a nursing home, there will be a scandal, they'll throw him out. One son says to the other, "Listen, I got an idea. They're making inflatable dolls now that are so fantastic you can't tell. And Papa doesn't see so well, he doesn't hear so well. It'll be fine."

The sons go and they spend a fortune on this blond, buxom blow-up doll. They put it in the bed, they bring their father in. They leave their father alone, they go outside and wait, and they hear a little noise—and all of a sudden, they hear an explosion, and the father screams. The sons run in and say, "Papa! What happened?"

The father says, "Well, this girl doesn't talk very much. So we're lying in bed, we're making out a little bit, I started to nibble a bit on her breast, and all of a sudden she farts and flies out the window!"

ALAN GORDON

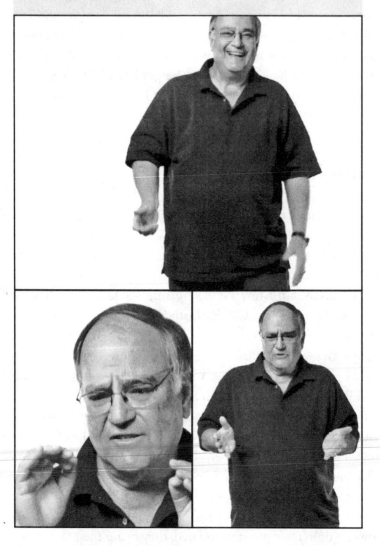

Alan Gordon was an executive at a local paper distribution company when I was in high school. Some of us worked for him in the summer. We rode around the massive warehouse on a pallet jack, picking loads for the trucks to deliver. We got a Teamsters card and overtime after 5 P.M. I used to try to remember all the words to "American Pie" as I rode around the warehouse. It helped pass the time.

Jake and Becky

Jake and Becky are an old couple. They've been dating for a while, and they decide "tonight's the night."

They get to her apartment and Jake says, "I gotta go to the bathroom."

He comes back out and there's Becky, standing on her head, legs akimbo, pants down, dress over her head.

"Becky, what are you doing?"

Becky says, "I figured, if you can't get it up, you can drop it in."

Joel Gorfinkel

"What's She Got?"

Morris and Becky are both in their eighties and are residing at the long-term care facility, the "Home," and have started a friendship.

Every Friday afternoon at 2:15 sharp Becky goes to Morris's room, closes the door, and just holds his penis for fifteen minutes. This goes on for four or five months.

One Friday at 2:15 sharp she shows up at Morris's room— no Morris. Panicked, she runs up and down the hall calling out, "Where's Morris, where's Morris?"

One of the attendants finally stops her and says, "Morris is down the hall in Zelda's room."

Becky goes down to Zelda's room, opens the door, and there sits Zelda with Morris, holding his penis. Becky cries out, "Morris, Morris, why are doing this? Haven't I been good enough for you? What does she have that I don't?"

Morris looks up at her and answers, *"Parkinson's disease!"*

Bernie Leibowitz

Sam and Molly

The following joke should be said (read) with a strong accent!

Sam and Molly are an old Jewish couple. Molly says, "Sam, get me some ice cream."

Sam says, "Okay."

Molly responds, "Sam, please write it down so you von't forget."

"I von't forget and I von't write it down!"

Molly says, "Okay, but vhile you're out, get me some pretzels, too. But Sam, please write it down so you von't forget!"

"I von't write it down and I von't forget!"

An hour later, Sam comes home. He opens the bag and takes out six bagels and a half-pound of lox.

Molly says, "Sam, didn't I tell you to write it down so you vouldn't forget? So vhere is the cream cheese?"

NORMAN STILES

During Norman Stiles's career on *Sesame Street,* he wrote more than one hundred scripts and conceived, co-conceived, or supervised the development of characters such as Count von Count, Forgetful Jones, Sonny Friendly, H. Ross Parrot, Placido Flamingo, Elmo, Telly Monster, the Amazing Mumford, Zoe, Rosita, etc.

Yes. Elmo.

Sperm Bank

So this ninety-eight-year-old man goes into a sperm bank and he says, "Excuse me, I would like to make a deposit."

And the nurse behind the counter says, "Okay, how old are you?"

"I'm ninety-eight. And if by that question, you are questioning whether I'm capable of making a deposit, you are sadly mistaken. You see, all my parts are in perfect working order. As my wife Sadie would attest, but she can't come here today because my parts are in such working order. She can't come here today because she's tired, understand? I want to make a deposit and I want to make it right now."

She says, "All right, all right, all right. Here's a jar; you go in that room. Would you need a magazine?"

"I don't need no magazines."

He goes in the room and about thirty seconds go by and the nurse hears "*Hyoyh. Hoooh. Hyeeeah. Ooooh.*"

"*WHOOOOA!*"

She goes and she knocks on the door and she says, "You all right?"

And he says, "I'm having trouble opening the jar."

Wayne Hochberg

Guess How Old

Morris and Sadie live in the same nursing home. Each day they take a walk down the hallway and often meet each other somewhere in the middle.

Usually they say a few things to each other and one day Morris says, "Sadie, today's my birthday. Wanna guess how old I am?"

Sadie says sure, then maneuvers her walker closer, reaches down, unzips his fly, pulls out his penis, and gives it a few wags. She then puts it back in his pants, rezips his fly, and says, "You're eighty-four."

Morris says, "That's amazing. How did you know?"

"You told me yesterday."

Jeff Loewi

Driving in Florida

Becky and Ethel are driving in Florida. Becky notices that Ethel has just run a red light but she decides to say nothing. Minutes later, Ethel runs another red light and Becky feels she must say something. "Ethel, do you realize you've just run two red lights?"

Ethel says, "I'm driving?"

George Bisacca

Multitasking

A ninety-year-old guy gets married for the third time to a younger woman.

After the wedding celebration they go out to the Hamptons to the cottage they have rented on the beach.

As they snuggle up to each other, the young wife begins to get excited and she whispers in his ear, "Sweetie, let's go upstairs and make love."

He looks at her and replies, "I can't do both."

Shelly Himmelfarb

Crazy Person

Eighty-five-year-old Hymie is driving down the highway when his cellphone rings. It's his wife in a panic, shouting, "Hymie, Hymie! Be careful! I just heard on the radio there's a crazy person driving the wrong way down the highway!"

Hymie says, "What do you mean one crazy person? There are hundreds!"

JOE SIMONOWITZ

Joe Simonowitz graduated from Samuel Gompers High School in the Bronx in 1949. The caption under his yearbook photo was "That reminds me of a joke."

A Death in the Family

This takes place in an old-age home.

Cohen has been in this old-age home for quite a while and has Alzheimer's. One of the nurses has taken a liking to him and always comes in to see how he is.

One day, she comes in to find him very sad; he is crying. She says, "Cohen, what happened?"

He says, "My penis died."

She doesn't pay him any mind.

The next day, he's walking up and down the aisles with his penis hanging out. The nurse grabs him, puts him back in his room, and says, "Mr. Cohen! You can't do that! Anyway, yesterday you told me your penis died!"

He says, "I know. Today's the viewing."

12

Death: The Last Laugh

What, You Want I Should Cry?

CHRISTIANS KNOW WHAT HAPPENS WHEN THEY DIE. THEIR philosophies of death and afterlife are abundantly disseminated—images of heaven and hell pervade classic Western art and literature and popular culture as well. But if you ask ten Jews what their religion suggests will happen after death, you'll get eleven different opinions.

So I went to the source, the unquestionable authority, the one Jew who always knows the answers: my mother. But she said, "Who wants to talk about death? It's depressing."

And essentially she's not far off from doctrinal philosophy.

I called an old friend, Dr. Abe Unger, who is both a rabbi and an academic, to pose the question to him: "What do the Jews think about death?" Rabbi Abe is an educated and contemplative man and his response surprised me. He said, "Well, the Jews don't actually talk about it a lot."

I wondered, Has he seen any of Woody Allen's thirty-nine movies? Jews I know are obsessed with death—and telling a lot of jokes about it, which indicates a profound cultural preoccupation.

But Rabbi Abe meant the philosophical Jews, the Jews who, throughout the past 3,500 years, have debated and written and evolved the Halakha, the collective body of Jewish religious law. He paraphrased the text *Halakhic Man,* by the theologian Rabbi Joseph Soloveitchik, who writes (and I paraphrase the paraphraser) that we fear and dread death because our duty is to do mitzvahs (our Halakhic obligations) and in death there is no opportunity to perform mitzvahs.

Interesting.

From what I gather, there are also limited opportunities to eat pizza, watch baseball, or get four-handed Thai massage.

But the message is clear—it's about now. It's not about earning frequent-flyer miles for a super-duper eternity. I mean, there is a Jewish heaven (all-you-can-eat-shrimp-poppers?) but apparently all the Jews get in. First you experience something like a Jewish version of purgatory, but after that, every single Semite is accepted.

This gave me an idea for a sequel to the 1989 animated film *All Dogs Go to Heaven* called, as you would expect, *All Hebes Go to Heaven*. But the recent Bernie Madoff scandal made me doubt this idea's veracity and I put off pitching this concept to Hollywood.

Actually, Rabbi Abe mentioned to me that, according to the Aristotelian medieval Jewish philosopher Maimonides, there could be a subtle meritocratic reward system in the afterlife—where the Jews who lived their lives more in accordance with Halacha would get to be closer to God after death. The Madoffs and their ilk wouldn't go to hell exactly but something like the Elizabeth, New Jersey, section of heaven.

The intellectual Jewish philosophies do dovetail with the armchair philosophies of the joke tellers in this chapter in one very important respect.

The bottom line is the same: Live it, love it, kiss it, hug it, laugh it, cry it, grab it, and squeeze it now while you can—because the only sure thing about death is the basket of rugelach at the shiva.

LARRY DONSKY

Larry Donsky and my father attended Camp Dellwood together in Honesdale, Pennsylvania, from 1950 to 1954. At camp, Larry was known as "Moose" Donsky. Later he played first base and catcher for a Coney Island League baseball team and worked in the Garment District in New York. He and my father fell out of touch for thirty years, until my father decided to look him up in the white pages and call him.

Hospital

I recently had to spend an evening at Center State Hospital and the guy in the bed next to me wasn't doing too well. Halfway into the night, the doctor came into the room, pulled the curtain between us, went over to the man and his wife, and said, "We've done all we can for you. You're not going to make it through the night. So all I suggest," he said to the wife, "is to try to make your husband as comfortable as possible."

He leaves, and it's about twelve o'clock at night and I can't sleep, I'm lying in my bed, and she says, "Darling, what can I do to make you more comfortable?"

And he says, "Well, I really don't feel all that bad. I'd really like to do it one more time."

She climbs into bed with him and I hear the bed going up and down, they're going at it for about forty minutes, finally they finish, she's moaning and groaning, and he says, "That was terrific."

She's sitting in the chair, it's now about one-thirty, and she says, "Darling, what can I do to make you more comfortable?"

He says, "I really feel great and I'd love to do it again."

It's about two-thirty in the morning; she jumps into the sack again. They go at it for about forty minutes. I can't believe it, I can't fall asleep, and he's moaning and groaning and it's wonderful.

Now it's about three-thirty in the morning. She says to him, "Darling, what can I do to make you more comfortable?"

He says, "You know, I really feel good. I'd like to do it one more time."

She looks at him and says, "Sure. You don't have to get up in the morning."

STEVE "SHECKY" PLATT

Steve Platt got divorced when he was fifty. When he decided to start dating, he placed an ad in *The Jewish Journal* that said, "50-year-old Unemployed Loser. I do not like movies, music, dancing, theater, arts, literature, dining, vacations, cruises, or walks on the beach." He received 183 responses.

Eulogies

This priest just finished this rousing sermon, which was about peace and love. He wheels around and he says to one of the congregants, "And you, sir, what would you like to hear them say as they walk past your casket?"

He says, "I'd like to hear them say that I was a hard worker; that I was a good provider; that I took care of my family."

"Thank you," says the priest. He points to another congregant. "And you, sir, what would you like to hear them say as they walk past your casket?"

He says, "I'd like to hear them say that I was a good father, a good husband, and a good brother, and that I contributed to the church."

"Thank you," says the priest. He points to another congregant. "And you, sir, what would you like to hear them say as they walk past your casket?"

He says, "I think I'd like to hear them say, 'Hey! I think he's moving!' "

JERRY BLOCK

Jerry Block sells commercial real estate. His appearance on our site wasn't his first time in front of the camera. A few years ago he was surreptitiously filmed while taking a New York City taxi and ended up in a Bud Lite commercial.

Heaven

They decided to change the rules for getting into heaven. Now when you reach the Pearly Gates, you have to tell the angel at the gates what it was like the day that you died.

Sure enough, the following day at noon, the first person shows up and the angel says, "Tell me, sir, what were the circumstances of your death?"

"I've often suspected my wife of cheating on me so I decided to come home early one afternoon. I happened to live on the twenty-fifth floor of this high-rise luxury apartment house, and as I walked in I noticed my wife was walking around without a stitch of clothing on. I became incensed.

"I walked around, I looked behind the couch, I looked behind the drapes, I didn't find anybody. I ran through the kitchen, and sure enough, right there on the patio, hanging from the ledge was some guy. I became so mad I jumped up, yelling and screaming at him. I took the heel of my shoe, I was banging it into his fingertips, and he fell to what I thought was certain death.

"But I took a look over the ledge, and sure enough, wouldn't you know, his fall was broken by a clump of bushes and he was looking up at me with this shit-eating grin on his face.

"So I ran back into the kitchen, hoping to find something to throw at him, and I spied the refrigerator. I rolled it out, I pushed it across the terrace, picked it up, pushed it over the side. It turned, end over end, and sure enough it just smashed him to smithereens. Well, the whole event was just too much for me to take. I had a massive heart attack and I died right there on the terrace."

The angel says, "Well, that certainly sounds like a crime of passion. Welcome to the kingdom of heaven. Next."

The next person shows up and the angel says, "Tell me, sir, what was it like on the day that you died?"

"Well, I happened to be exercising in my apartment this afternoon. I happened to live on the twenty-sixth floor of this high-rise luxury apartment house. It was a little too warm inside the apartment so I decided to drag my equipment out, and I'm jumping up and down on my trampoline on the terrace, and sure enough I jumped right off it and I put my hands out, hoping to grab anything to break my fall and I did grab on to the terrace of the floor beneath me.

"This madman came out onto the terrace, yelling and screaming and banging away. He jumped up on the terrace and with the heel of his shoe he banged on my fingertips until I couldn't hold on any longer and I fell to what I thought was certain death, except my fall was broken by this clump of bushes.

"I was looking up at the sky, thanking God, smiling that He had spared me, when all of a sudden I saw this madman take what looked like a refrigerator, he pushed it over the edge and it fell end over end, hit me, smashed me to smithereens, and that's how I died."

The angel thinks for a minute and says, "That too sounds like a crime of passion. Welcome to the kingdom of heaven. Next."

Next man shows up and the angel says, "Tell me, sir, what was it like on the day you died? What were the circumstances of your death?"

And the gentleman looks him straight in the face and says, "Well, picture this. There I was hiding in this refrigerator . . ."

Benjamin Dreyer

Rugelach

The old man is dying.

He calls his son into his bedroom. "Sammy," he says, "I can smell all the way up here that your mother is downstairs in the kitchen, baking rugelach. You know that your mother's rugelach is my favorite thing in the world. I'm sure that this will be the last thing I'll ever eat. Would you please go downstairs and get me some?"

Sammy leaves the room.

Five minutes go by. Ten minutes.

Fifteen minutes later, Sammy returns to his father's bedroom. Empty-handed.

"Sammy," the old man says, "where's the rugelach?"

"Pop," Sammy says sheepishly, "Mom says they're for after the funeral."

BARNETT HOFFMAN

When I was a boy and my father was in the prosecutor's office, he received a death threat from an escaped convict. We had an armed bodyguard stay overnight in our living room. He helped me untangle my fishing rod.

Medium

Jake dies.

Becky goes to one of those mediums and the medium looks into her crystal ball and a voice comes out. "Becky."

She says, "Is that you, Jake?"

"It's me, Becky."

"Really? How is it, Jake?"

"Oh, Becky, it's wonderful. Every day I wake up, the first thing I do in the morning is have sex. And then I have some breakfast. And then I take a little nap. Sex again. And then lunch. And then a nap. And then I have sex, snack, and then I take another nap. Sex, nap, food, wonderful. And I do this seven days a week."

"Jake, you're so lucky. Heaven must be wonderful."

"Who's in heaven? I'm in a bull in Montana."

CHUCK BERKE

Chuck Berke moved to Del Mar, California, twenty years ago and has been a real estate broker there ever since.

The Accident

A little Jewish lady was not very attractive—in fact, she was awful looking—and had lived a somewhat unlucky, sad, and lonely life. One day she is on a crowded bus and there's an accident. She is apparently mortally wounded and on the way to the hospital, she thinks, Again unlucky, and now I'm about to die.

While she is pondering her sad life before she expires, God suddenly appears before her and says, "I know you've had a tough life but I'm not ready to take you. Also, you'll receive an ample sum for your injuries—it should easily last you for the twenty more years of life you'll have!"

She's overjoyed with the opportunity to finally enjoy life and figures that she might as well give herself the best opportunity. So, while still in the hospital, she gets cosmetic surgery for her face and entire body. After months of treatments and recovery, she looks in the mirror and sees that she is beautiful!

She leaves the hospital and gets in a taxi to go home. The taxi has a serious accident with another car and the woman feels her life ebbing away. Suddenly, God appears again. She says, "How could this happen? You told me that I would have another twenty years of life!"

God replies, "Oh shit! I didn't recognize you!"

DANIEL OKRENT

Dan Okrent served for eighteen months as the first public editor of *The New York Times.*

Tommy the Cat

This is about Max and Morris, who are brothers in the shmata business, and they've been partners for years. Max has got a family, and Morris lives alone with his cat, Tommy.

And one day Max says to his brother, "Morris, you've just been working much too hard. You gotta take a vacation. You gotta get away from the business for a bit."

Morris says, "How can I do that? Who's gonna take care of my cat? Tommy the cat? I love him so much, I can't be away from him."

Max says, "I'll take care of Tommy the cat."

Morris says, "You'd do that for me?"

Max says, "Of course I'd do that for you. I'm your brother. You go have a nice time. Go to Miami. Have a nice trip."

So Morris gets on a plane, he flies down. Soon as he gets off the plane, he gets out his cellphone and he calls up his brother. He says, "So Max, I'm in Miami. How's Tommy the cat?"

Max says, "Well, Tommy the cat, he went for a walk on the roof, and he fell off. He's dead."

Morris says, "What are you saying to me?"

Max says, "I'm saying Tommy the cat went for a walk on the roof; he fell off. He's dead."

Morris says, "I can't believe this. Max, how can you say this? This cat, this little guy, he means so much to me. You just tell me like this? You've got to learn how to break it to me gentle when you tell me something like that."

Max says, "What do you mean, 'break it to you gentle'?"

Morris says, "Well, this is what you should do: I get off the plane, I call you. I'd say, 'How's Tommy the cat?' You'd say, 'Oh, he's got a little sniffle.'

"Then the next day, I'd check into the Fontainebleau. I'd get up in the morning; before I've even had my breakfast, I'd give you a call. I'd say, 'So nu? With Tommy the cat and the sniffles?'

"You'd say, 'Well, he got a little raspy in his chest, so I thought I'd take him to the hospital. But, you know, everything's going to be okay. He's a great little cat; the nurses love him.'

"And the next day, I'd go out and maybe play some shuffleboard, talk to the ladies. I call and again, I say, 'So nu with Tommy the cat?'

"And you'd say to me something like 'Well, you know, it's a little touch-and-go, but I think he's going to be okay. But just to be sure, we brought in a great cat man from Chicago. He's going to take a good look at him and everything's going to be all right.'

"Then the next day, I'd call and say, 'Nu with the cat man from Chicago?'

"And you'd say, 'Well, I hate to tell you this, Morris, but it's not a happy ending. Tommy the cat was a great little cat, and he struggled, he fought, he was so courageous, but in the end he expired. They'd never seen a cat like this with such bravery. You should be proud.'

"So you see, when I go through a tragedy like this, don't say, 'Tommy the cat, he went for a walk on the roof, he fell off. He's dead.' You break it to me gentle, you understand?"

Max says, "Okay, I understand, I understand."

"Good, now that you understand, so tell me, how's Mom?"

Max says, "Well, she's got a little sniffle."

Marty Angstreich

Grief

So a man is walking through a cemetery when off in the distance he hears someone wailing, "Oy why did you die, oy why?"

As he walks closer, he sees the voice is coming from an elderly gentleman in a black yarmulke, praying at a gravestone and repeating over and over again, "Oy why did you die, oy why? Oy why did you die, oy why?"

The man goes up to the mourner and says, "Excuse me, sir, I don't want to bother you in your time of grief, but the deceased must have been a dear loved one."

The mourner cries, "No, I didn't even know him!"

"You didn't know him? Then who is it?"

The elderly gentleman replies in wails and tears, "It was my wife's first husband! Oy why did you die, oy why?"

Dr. Josh Backon

Opening Night

It's opening night on Broadway and the scalpers are having a field day; no tickets are to be had.

A middle-aged couple sees that next to them is a little old Jewish lady sitting next to an empty seat.

The man asks, "Whose seat is that?" and the old lady replies, "My late husband, Irving Bernstein."

He says, "I'm sorry but surely you must have some friends or relatives who would have wanted to come and see the show!"

She replies, "Yes, but they're all at the funeral."

A Final Bonus Freudian Knock-Knock Joke

"Knock knock."

"Who's there?"

"Vienna."

"Vienna who?"

"Vienna city in Austria. Vere did you think ve vere?"

Special Added Bonus Chapter

A Joke About Jokes

MICHAEL MILLER

For a comedy sketch on *The Late Late Show*, Michael Miller portrayed a drummer playing rim shots for an AARP comedian. Ringo Starr told him he was "fantastic." Not a bad review for the first and last time he ever played the drums.

Jokes in Prison

This guy goes to prison. He's very scared.

The first day he's eating lunch, and when lunch is over he sees one of the inmates get up on the table and say, "Thirty-two!" and everybody in the whole place laughs. And then he says, "Sixty-eight!" and people are roaring.

The new prisoner says to the guy next to him, "What's going on?"

The guy next to him says, "Well, you know, we've all been here so long, we've heard all the jokes. We've memorized them, so we don't have to retell them. We just say the number, and people remember it, and then they laugh."

Well, this guy just thinks that's terrific. So he spends the entire next year memorizing and practicing all of the jokes.

He's finally ready and he gets the nerve to try it. He stands up on the table and shouts, "Fifty-five!"

Dead silence. He can't believe it. He thinks for a moment and says, "Seventy-four!"

Again the room is completely still. The other inmates stare at him. He starts to panic. So he picks the surefire one.

He says, "One hundred and three!"

Nothing happens.

He goes back to his seat. He says to the guy next to him, "What happened? What went wrong?"

The guy says, "Well, some people can tell a joke, and some people just can't."

Acknowledgments

The authors would like to acknowledge the following people, without whom this book would not be possible. Tim Williams, not only the most fundamentally decent man we'll probably ever meet, but also one of the most Waspy, gets honorary Hebe status for his tireless efforts in support of this project. John Penotti, Mike Hogan, and Peter Block at Greenestreet Films/A Bigger Boat were always upbeat and encouraging. Kate Lee at ICM helped us, a couple of publishing greenhorns, find a home. Thanks to Jill Schwartzman, our editor at Random House, who manages to be so nice even when she doesn't like something. To Jon Podwil, for his game-changing work on the photographs, and to Antonio Rossi for his beautiful cinematography and his quiet chuckling behind the camera when the punch lines hit.

Sam, specifically, would like to thank his wife, Andrea, for her sly wit, constant support, and irrepressible honesty. He also thanks his mother for picking the exact right time to finally get a joke right and his father for the incomparable genetic gift of humor. He offers gratitude also to his parents' extended community for their generous cooperation and wonderful jokes. Finally, he would like to thank Eric Spiegelman for his steadfast partnership, for being outrageously good at picking his battles, and for knowing so much stuff about the Internets.

Eric specifically thanks Tim Williams for believing in him, and, at the risk of being redundant, Sam Hoffman, who just totally knocked this one out of the park. He owes gratitude to a few other people as well: His dad for having an uncompromising sense of humor, which constantly forces Eric to raise his game, comedically speaking. His mom for doing everything she can to lend support (she even chipped in at the craft services table during production!). Mike Hudack at blip.tv, whose support for the video series was essential to its success. Liana Maeby for her constant encouragement and for generally putting up with him.

Both authors would like to recognize, appreciate, and applaud the American Jewish culture, which has elevated storytelling and laughter to the centerpiece of its very existence.

About the Authors

During a twenty-year career in the New York film industry, SAM HOFFMAN has produced, directed, or assistant-directed numerous films, shorts, second units, and commercials, including *The Royal Tenenbaums, The School of Rock, The Producers* (musical), *Donnie Brasco, Dead Man Walking,* and *Groundhog Day.* Currently, Hoffman is executive-producing *The Oranges,* starring Hugh Laurie and Catherine Keener.

In January 2009, Hoffman partnered with Jetpack Media to launch OldJewsTellingJokes.com—a website devoted to video portraits of old Jews telling jokes. Since then, the videos have been viewed more than 7 million times and have been released on DVD by First Run Features. The site, covered by countless blogs, has been featured in *New York* magazine, The Huffington Post, and *The Wall Street Journal.*

Hoffman graduated with honors from the University of Pennsylvania. He lives in New York City with his wife, Andrea Crane, a modern art specialist with the Gagosian Gallery, and their son, Jack, and daughter, Juliet.

ERIC SPIEGELMAN produces original Internet content for Jetpack Media, a production company founded by GreeneStreet Films in 2008. Before that, he was a lawyer. Spielgelman graduated from the University of California Hastings College of the Law and from Boston University. He lives in the Silver Lake neighborhood of Los Angeles.

About the Type

This book was set in Bembo, a typeface based on an old-style Roman face that was used for Cardinal Bembo's tract *De Aetna* in 1495. Bembo was cut by Francisco Griffo in the early sixteenth century. The Lanston Monotype Machine Company of Philadelphia brought the well-proportioned letter forms of Bembo to the United States in the 1930s.